Breaking Your Neck is a Pain in the Butt

How I Handled Life's Challenges with Grace and Humor

by Cherie Cotner

ISBN 978-1-63885-566-8 (Paperback)
ISBN 978-1-63885-567-5 (Digital)

Thank you to my niece, Dani Ostrowski for creating my cover art.

Covenant Books
11661 Hwy 707
Murrells Inlet, SC 29576
www.covenantbooks.com

In memory of my mother in heaven, Martha Jane Dixon,
who always demonstrated what a smile can do

To my daughters, Carissa and Cailey, who are gifts from God. They have blessed me with much joy and fulfillment. Exceptions to the "pain the butt."

FOREWORD

Consider it pure joy, my brothers, whenever you face trials of any kind (James 1:2).

I decided on the title for my book in 1991, when "normal" did not apply to my lifestyle anymore. It is hard to believe it has taken me thirty-six years to finally publish it. When I got out of the rehabilitation hospital in 1984, at Christmas, I found it was more difficult to write numerous personalized Christmas cards sharing the same stories and basically saying the same thing. I began writing a single letter and printing it out on red or green paper and sending to all my family and friends. Many who have received my Christmas letters over the numerous years will recognize the stories; however, there will be more details and narrative that could not be described in my letters. I did not set out to write a book until the people reading my Christmas letters kept remarking that they enjoyed my letters and said I should write a book. During the early years of my disability, things were more difficult and oftentimes inconvenient, so my title of the book came as a natural consequence.

When I thought of the title *Pain in the Butt*, it meant figuratively, since I do not even have sensation there! Ironically, I do have a constant numbness in my butt and lower extremities which drives me crazy! I finally was prescribed medication years ago to alleviate some of it; however, the tingling is a constant in my life. As I have shared my title with people through the years, the reaction is always a laugh, as I had hoped to invoke humor. I wrote it with that in mind. I hope once you read my book, you will see despite the turn my life took on that fateful day in December, I not only survived the tragedy but went on to live an exuberant and joyful life, "joie de vivre."

Sometimes, when something bad happens, you may think it is the end of your life, which I could have easily done. However, I think of all my accomplishments from the past thirty-six years. If I had given up at the beginning, I would not have achieved my greatest accomplishments—the birth of my two daughters! Many people do not realize there were not too many quadriplegic women having babies back in 1989 or even 1992. I had to seek out a young girl back in the '80s who had done so, but I think she was paraplegic. It was always fun when people asked me how long I had been in the wheelchair when the girls were young. They could see from their ages that I had given birth after my spinal cord injury and would show astonishment.

I hope this book will help others who have either suffered through a tragedy or know someone who did and want to share this book with them. I do not have all the answers, but I am sharing my experiences and how I dealt with the tough issues. This is my story, based on my memories I have shared over the years in my Christmas letters. In publishing my story, my hope is you can find joy despite disability, loss, or any tragedy that befalls you or a loved one. I can feel proud that when I pass on, I have been the best role model possible. I believe God will be pleased and say, "Well done, faithful daughter!"

CHAPTER ONE

In the Blink of an Eye

December 16, 1983, 6:00 p.m.

In a moment, my life was tragically altered on a beautiful winter night. In this story, the first snow of the season had melted; the sun had shined bright all day. For the most part, it was just another normal workday; however, being a Friday, it meant the weekend rush of getting out of town. Unfortunately, the rush began about the same time the sun was setting, and the beautiful snow melted into ice on the bridges in Grandview, Texas. My husband, Stephen, and I had stopped briefly at a drugstore, running in to pick up birth control, not knowing that these would be my last steps! This perfectly normal workday suddenly changed to tragedy in a matter of seconds for a newlywed couple of only six months, as we crossed a bridge with one small patch of black ice. The black ice met with the tire of our new Datsun 280ZX resulting in Stephen losing control of the powerful vehicle at fifty-five miles per hour, flipping our car over the guardrail, and rolling down a thirty-foot embankment. Stephen was thrown to the backseat, cushioned by the Christmas presents in transport. I was not so fortunate. Propelled through the sunroof, I landed on the ice-covered ground, severing the seventh vertebrae of my spinal cord. On December 16, 1983, the accident thus altered my life in the time it takes to blink, when thrown from the car.

My severed spine resulted in immediate paralysis and loss of sensation which prevented me from feeling the additional critical injuries that night. The top of my scalp was sliced from my head (leaving me with months of bad hair days) and a compound fracture of the arm with a nasty scar as a reminder. If I had been cognitively aware of either of these injuries, I'm convinced I would not have survived the accident. I do not have much memory of going over the bridge and what emotions I was experiencing. I wish I could have seen pictures of the accident site or what the car looked like after the crash. I would still shudder at the thought of what occurred there when I have crossed that bridge in later years.

It's interesting what you remember during moments of trauma. I was dozing off with our cat, Dudley, on my lap at the moment of impact. The first thing I remember hearing was the car audio system stating in a women's voice, "The emergency brake is on!" Next, I remember hearing other cars sounding as though they were coming down the embankment, and I feared a car crushing me, as if I didn't have enough trouble already! The ground was freezing cold, and all I wanted was to be moved to a warm, safe spot. Being a health education major at Texas A&M University, I knew the logic of not moving an accident victim. Unfortunately, my logic fled the moment panic set in. I begged Stephen to move me from the icy ground. Later, he believed he bore some guilt about moving me and possibly causing more damage to the spine. The doctor assured him the damage was already done. I drifted in and out of consciousness that night. One of the most difficult tasks of the evening was for Stephen to contact my mother about the accident. We were on our way to visit her in Anderson, Texas, the weekend before Christmas. Our sports car was packed with Christmas gifts, which my mom was planning to transport to Houston, Texas, where the Dixon clan planned to spend the Christmas holiday the following week. The area code had changed recently in Anderson, Texas, so Stephen prodded me in one of my conscious moments and was surprised I was able to recall the new area code.

My regret in Stephen having to make that phone call to my mom was it followed the tragedy of my Father's death by only fifteen months. I can't imagine what she suffered the night of my accident.

My dad had died of a sudden heart attack the previous September, throwing the whole family into a tailspin. When my sister Karen came to my apartment door the night of September 19, 1982, to give me the news, I thought she was going to say our grandfather had died. I was literally in shock for several weeks from this unexpected tragedy. I felt cheated as my dad and I were just beginning to enjoy an adult relationship. One thing which gave me comfort about his death was at a recent funeral. It was a comment from the pastor discussing a man who had died and had similar beliefs in education to my dad. She said simply, "Now he (the man who died) knows more than we do." Knowing my dad is up in heaven, probably in deep discussions with God, made me smile and feel closer to them both.

I was taken by ambulance to the closest major hospital, which was Campbell Memorial in Cleburne, Texas. I have no memory of my time at this hospital; although I've been told this was where my broken arm was attended to. I was told my clothes were cut off to assess my injuries. My mother always ingrained in me that you always put your face (makeup) and clean underwear on before leaving the house. I knew I had on makeup but am embarrassed to admit I can't remember if my underwear was clean. In hindsight, it is a silly thing to worry about. That was the least of least of my worries!

My more critical injuries would need to be addressed in a larger, more acute care hospital. The weather was too tenuous to have me airlifted to Harris Hospital in Ft. Worth. I was driven by ambulance once again, and it was during this ride I was abruptly told by the medic that he had seen these types of injuries before, stating I would never walk again. I'm sure any psychology student could tell you I didn't need to hear this just then! That stands out in my recollection of being told the ominous statement "You will never walk again" more than anything official from the doctors. I didn't break down with hysterics or cry out, "Why me?" I just remember this foreboding conversation in the ambulance.

If you ever get depressed during the holidays, I recommend you think of people in the hospital or other dire circumstances, and your holiday blues will become a holiday blessing! I know because this is where I spent the Christmas of '83. What should have been one of the happiest memories of my newlywed year turned into one of the most depressing moments in my life. Amazingly enough, most of our Christmas gifts had been recovered from the accident. Only a few small boxes were not found and were probably treasures found by some lucky homeless person hiking along the freeway. I appreciated the efforts made by my family to make my Christmas more pleasant. However, no matter how much you decorate a hospital room, the spirit just isn't the same. You are stuck there in the hospital while everyone else leaves to continue with their festivities. If I can ever remember a moment of self-pity, it was when everyone left to go home.

I also thought about how I would return to work with a disability. Richard Wilson from the Carter Blood Center assured me my job would be waiting when I returned. I learned later he went out on a limb, so to speak, to make this guarantee, especially since he had only known me for six months. I admire how he was willing to overlook all the obstacles I was facing and believed in my ability to get back to work after such a major injury.

*My life lesson 1: Appreciate every moment in life
because you never know what may happen.*

Thirty-foot embankment
we rolled down

Wedding picture, July 9, 1983

Bridge that changed my life
7 Granbury, Texas,
December 16, 1983
Grandview

CHAPTER TWO

Don't Have a Cow—I Do Have a Cat

St. Paul Hospital, Dallas, January 1984

Our cat fled the scene—truly depicting the expression "scaredy-cat." I know he must have been freaked with all the noise, confusion, and bad weather. He always had a cautious nature. Frankly, I did not remember much about this, but I know I had family members who were on the task of scouting the area the next day for Dudley. One helpful animal lover stated Dudley would not surface until the weather warmed up from the record freezing temperatures we were experiencing. Her prediction proved accurate almost a month later!

It was not only the physical aspect of the accident I was suffering those initial months; it was an emotional blow to lose my beloved cat. I'd had Dudley since he was a kitten during my senior year at Texas A&M several years before my accident. I agonized over what had happened to Dudley and how he might be suffering. In some way, it took the focus off my situation. I have always been more concerned for others than myself.

When I was relapsing with a pulmonary clot in January, I was feeling very strange but could not explain what was happening. I was hallucinating. I felt as though I was floating at the ceiling in my bed. I was told I talked about my cat, Dudley, who disappeared at the accident site. Friends and family were still checking the accident site for signs of him, but nothing yet. I told the nurses that Dudley was there with me.

I believe I was more in danger of dying from the pulmonary embolism[1] that day than on the day of the accident. I don't recall my hospitalization at St. Paul other than what I've been told. I believe I was taken there by ambulance, operated on within hours, and returned to the rehab hospital within a day or two. Even though I was close to death, I don't recall seeing a "light" or getting a visit from my dad. I guess it wasn't my time yet, but I sure miss my dad and would have enjoyed a pep talk.

There was no pep talk, but maybe my dad had something to do with Dudley showing back up almost a month later, when the weather was considerably warmer. Dudley went up to a house in the area and still had his collar and tags intact. I believe the veterinarian's phone number was on the rabies tag, and after receiving the call as to his whereabouts, he called Stephen about Dudley being found. A few days later, Stephen came into my room at the rehab and pulled Dudley out from beneath his overcoat! He was not happy to be smuggled in under the coat—too undignified for a cat, but I could not think of a better omen for my future

My life lesson 2: Don't lose faith in what you believe.

Dudley, 1981–1998

CHAPTER THREE

I'm a Quad, but Don't Tell Anyone

Dallas Rehab, Dallas, Texas, 1983

My neck was severed at what the medical community calls C-6-7, an incomplete injury. The spine ranges from the cervical to the thoracic, down to the lumbosacral; and my injury was unfortunately in the cervical region which technically labeled me as quadriplegic. Many people mistakenly believe I'm paraplegic because my fingers are straight, and the movement of my wrists gives the impression that I'm using my hands.

Let me explain (more details on levels located in Notes[2]): there are several levels of function in a spinal cord injury, ranging from a C1 injury to T-12. Depending on where your injury occurred on the spine, your symptoms and the effects on your body differ. The higher up on the spine the injury occurred, the more severe your injury will be.

Cervical (neck) injuries usually result in full or partial tetraplegia (quadriplegia)1. However, depending on the specific location and severity of trauma, limited function may be retained.

- Injuries at the C-1/C-2 levels will often result in loss of breathing, necessitating mechanical ventilators or phrenic nerve pacing.
- C3 vertebrae and above typically results in loss of diaphragm function, necessitating the use of a ventilator for breathing.
- C4 results in significant loss of function at the biceps and shoulders.

- C5 results in potential loss of function at the shoulders and biceps, and complete loss of function at the wrists and hands.
- C6 (my level) results in limited wrist control and complete loss of hand function
- C7 and T1 result in lack of dexterity in the hands and fingers but allows for limited use of arms. My fingers look normal, but I have no muscle movement and no ability to grip.

I had an incomplete injury, which means there is still some function below the point of my injury. While a complete injury affects both sides of the body equally, an incomplete injury may affect both sides differently. The patient may be able to move a limb on one side of the body more than the other. Depending on which part of the spinal cord was injured (such as the back, front, side, or center), the effects will differ. In my case, I could not feel a pin prick on my arm; however, if you brushed me with a soft feather across my hand, I could feel this sensation. Fortunately for me, the spinal cord does not take all signals from the brain—independently controlling involuntary processes in the bowel, kidneys, and bladder.

Even to this day, I'm perplexed by the complexities of the spinal cord. In modern terms, the spinal cord is like the internet, sensitive tissue neurons that run down the backbone connecting the brain to the rest of the body sending out vital nerve signals. In my case, the signal has been disrupted, resulting in the loss of sensory feeling and ability to control movement

I compare my spinal cord and messaging center to a game I used to play as a child called "Red Rover." We would stand in two lines facing one another with our hands clasped tightly. Then one player would yell, "Red Rover, Red Rover, let Cherie come over!" I would look for the weakest link and race across and try to break through their arms. Sometimes, I could break through, sometimes not. That is what I think my spinal cord is like now. Many messages prevented from getting through those darned clasped arms!

Unfortunately, we have tough lessons in life. One is the fact we do not appreciate things in our life until we lose them. This may apply to people or in my case my body. I never fully appreciated my ability to run five miles. I took it for granted and never thought it could be altered so suddenly. I have discovered a new appreciation for the abilities I have developed in the past thirty-seven years.

My life lesson 3: Appreciate every small function of your body. It is a true sign of God's glory.

CHAPTER FOUR

It Could Be Worse

Harris Hospital, Ft. Worth, Texas, January 1984

I was initially put on a bed, called a Stryker Frame, which turned me facing straight up at the ceiling or facing straight down at the floor, and where flipping back and forth every two to three hours was always a frightening experience. If you required cervical traction (device that stretches the neck to reduce pressure on the spine) in the days before halos and early surgical stabilization, this was done with traction applied through tongs screwed into your head just above your ears. A rope went from the tongs through a special pulley installed in the pivot point of the Stryker Frame so as you were turned, the bed and you were essentially pivoted around the rope. The traction both kept the spine aligned while it healed, and reduced muscle spasms to hopefully allow dislocated bones to slip back into their normal position. Fortunately, I had no feeling or sensation during this experience. I was given a mirror to use to view family and friends when they visited. I instantly recalled the movie *The Other Side of the Mountain*, a true story about Jill Kilmont, who was paralyzed in a skiing accident. I never imagined when I watched the movie that a few years later I would be in the same situation. I was then moved to a bed called a Roto-Rest or "Pulmonaire," which constantly rotated me forty degrees to each side to prevent skin breakdown as well as pneumonia (keeping the lung secretions moving). When friends and family visited, they would have to move from side to side if they wanted to speak to my face. Fortunately, it moved very slowly and didn't wear anyone out! This was an improvement over having to lie down on the floor to speak to me.

My hospital stay was two weeks—probably the longest two weeks in my life. It was an emotional one, since it was during the holidays and a physical one, as I was constantly suctioned to prevent my lungs from filling and resulting in pneumonia. The purpose of tracheal/endotracheal suction is to remove pulmonary secretions in patients who are unable to cough and clear their own secretions effectively. As a result of remaining sedentary for over a week, my congestion grew worse as the days passed. My mother felt the nurses were rather rough in their breathing treatments and screamed at anyone who would listen to her. As I remember, they would hold me down and cover both my mouth and nose, which prevented any breathing on my part. I know the treatments were necessary, but I'm glad my mother eventually got the approval that only respiratory therapists would do my treatments. A first of many moments I would be thankful to have family and friends looking out for me.

It was then decided I would be transferred to what was then the Dallas Rehabilitation Hospital (DRI). Stephen worked on the insurance end to get me admitted. It was tricky getting me admitted as the insurance company was claiming I was not covered! I had just started at Carter Blood Center, as a Community Relations Coordinator, and insurance could not be obtained until six months. Thank God, Stephen's dad ingrained upon him you should always have insurance coverage. He purchased a temporary policy in which the insurance agent said we could pay in two payments. Stephen fortunately paid the second payment on December 13, three days prior to my accident! The check was also cashed prior to my accident, so my insurance payment went through (even though the insurance agent was wrong in allowing two payments). If the check had not been cashed, it might have turned out more problematic for me. It also worked to my favor. The computers were down at DRI, and my insurance couldn't be verified the day I was admitted. I felt as though I was smuggled into the rehab. I imagine the insurance agent was fired for his mistake, as my rehabilitation cost $150,000 or more. My policy was for five years or $500,000, whichever came first. Surprisingly, the five years came first.

Once again, I was admitted during the holiday. This was the New Year's holiday, welcoming me into 1984. It wasn't going to be a big celebration for me; however, I learned from seeing others in the rehab hospital, it could be much worse. I remember not wanting Stephen to take me on a tour when I was first able to sit up in a wheelchair because "I wasn't like them!" I saw people walking around with halos (neck braces) on their necks—looking like Frankenstein, or others rolling flat on beds for pressure relief. I just couldn't face reality at first that I was like these other folks in rehabilitation and this was my future. However, the scar on the front of my neck didn't seem so freakish anymore compared to the halo.

As I got around and met the other patients, I discovered they were just like me—there because of a tragic accident resulting in spinal cord accident, head injuries or both. I was blessed not to have sustained a head injury; although I was followed closely for several weeks to see if I displayed any symptoms, such as difficulty concentrating, mood swings, or prolonged confusion. I took several personality and memory tests, just to make certain.

Despite my fears, it is in my nature to make friends. As a child, I was assertive. My mom said when we moved to our house on Holly Grove in Houston (I was about five years old), I went door-to-door looking for friends my age. This continued throughout my teenage years and was voted "Most Popular" during my junior year of high school. I was never good at math, so when I was asked to count backward or multiply by seven until they said stop, it wasn't surprising that it was difficult. I don't remember being ranked in my class, but it was somewhere around the middle. I managed to graduate from both high school and college with decent grade averages. Although after my first year in college at Texas A&M, my dad sat me down and relayed in his thoughtful but firm way that I was in college to learn but my grade point average was not reflecting this. He encouraged me to aim for a 3.0 grade point average by the time I graduated and if I made the goal, he would put a diamond in my Aggie ring. I am so glad he saw me reach that goal, 3.033. He died the following year,

19

but I still remember his excitement over my achieving this goal. The diamond is a wonderful reminder of my hard work and his reward.

One young woman, who was not so fortunate, remains in my memory as her story is more tragic than mine. She was on the way to her bridal shower when she was hit by an eighteen-wheeler. Her head injury destroyed the future she had dreamed of, because she lost all memory of those she loved and details of her life. One important tidbit I learned while in rehabilitation is that there is always someone in worse shape than you are. It makes it more difficult to feel sorry for yourself and easier to be grateful for what you have. My blessings consisted of (1) no brain injury, (2) wrist movement which allowed me to use hand splints to eat or write, (3) a husband who came every day to see me, (4) a supportive family who took turns visiting, and (5) my life! Need I say more?

I didn't realize getting into a wheelchair, after lying in a hospital bed for two weeks, would be such an ordeal; but I could not stay upright for more than five minutes without passing out. My blood pressure would plummet; and there I would go, slumped over in the wheelchair—held in with a seatbelt to prevent me falling to the floor. I finally got outfitted for a "girdle type" apparatus that would bind my middle and keep my blood pressure from falling. Before I could start therapy, I had to be able to sit up. Just as I was getting better at staying in an upright position, I had a relapse. Little did I know but a blood clot had dislodged from my lower body and traveled upward. As I briefly mentioned in chapter 2, I was feeling very strange but could not explain what was happening. I was hallucinating. I felt as though I was floating at the ceiling above my bed. When I was talking to others, I couldn't explain how I felt. My father-in-law visited during that time and was saying, "You're doing so well!" Inside my head, I just wanted to scream, "No, I'm not!" Fortunately, my mom came to visit and noticed immediately that I did not look well and brought my condition to the attention of nearby nurses. I'm not sure of the time line, but within minutes of her visit, I was hemorrhaging through the nose, and I was rushed to St. Paul's Methodist Hospital. It was a blood clot to the lung. The technical term is a pulmonary embolism. I was operated on, and they put in a "Greenfield

Filter,"[3] which would prevent further blood clots from rising. I was very fortunate that day—the clot could have traveled to my heart or my brain. The Greenfield Filter has held up for over thirty years! I never knew the doctor who operated on me that day, but years later, he happened to be at a church board meeting in which I gave a devotional (included in book). The doctor came up and introduced himself after the meeting as the doctor who operated on me at St. Paul. I believe it made him happy to see how well it all turned out for me against tough odds or, as Paul Harvey always said, "here's the rest of the story."

My life lesson 4: You may think it looks greener on the other side of the fence, but you should be happy where you are!

CHAPTER FIVE

Rebuilding Confidence with Therapy

Dallas Rehab, February–May 1984

Once I was strong enough to get back in the wheelchair and stay upright, I was ready to begin my therapies—physical, occupational, respiratory, and behavioral medicine (counseling). The first three therapies were repeated twice daily, five times per week and a half day on Saturdays. Behavioral medicine was once a day, only on weekdays. I protested fiercely at the beginning that I did not need counseling. However, as the days progressed, I discovered it was better to talk about my feelings and about the many changes in my life.

Physical therapy was like starting as a baby with no balance. My first days in physical therapy consisted of being placed on an exercise mat and my therapist, Susan, shoving at each shoulder to see if I could stay upright. I would topple over like a five-month-old baby when I began physical therapy. That is when I realized I was essentially starting from scratch. I had a hard time at the beginning as my blood pressure was so low, but I slowly got to where I could withstand the prodding from the therapist. The therapist told me it would take the full five months that I was expected to stay in rehabilitation to build up my strength. I'm not sure how I compare to people with similar injuries, but to this day, I really don't have great balance and friends laugh with me when I slip from my armrests. I know I must look as ridiculous as I feel, so it's easier to laugh at myself. I often scare people who are not accustomed to this behavior, as they think I'm falling out of my chair.

I would then go to occupational therapy. Occupational therapists use treatments to develop, recover, or maintain the daily living and work skills of their patients with a physical, mental, or developmental condition. My earliest memories are of performing arm exercises to Michael Jackson tunes. I also got comic relief from fellow patients, like Greg (a fellow quadriplegic), who grabbed my attention when he was exercising and singing, "Grow little boobies, bigger, bigger so I can have a better figure, figure!" With spinal cord injuries, you lose muscle tone. He was just making fun since there was nothing he could do to change his physique. I admired him for his sense of humor and ability to make fun of himself and decided I was going to strive to do this as well. My therapist, Kathy, then introduced me to former patient Natalie, who performed effortlessly at some tasks I never could imagine being able to do. She was a true inspiration whom I still admire to this day. She could push from a manual wheelchair, which looked effortlessly to me. She could transfer independently to a bed or chair, which I've never been able to do. I believe it has something to do with my short arm span. It was impossible for me to grab underneath my legs and lift them over to another surface. Natalie could also get herself into a swimming pool and swim independently. And last and most impressive, she could get into a regular car and slide her wheelchair into the backseat! There was a new show out then called *Push Girls*. Natalie was the true definition of a "Push Girl." Their motto was "If you can't stand up, stand out." I've got the attitude but not the physical ability for a manual wheelchair. I kept in touch with Natalie while I lived in Ft. Worth but lost contact once I moved to Houston. What I have learned over the years is that people with spinal cord injuries vary as much as "normal" people do in terms of ability, strength, and emotional stability. A pivotal moment came when I was being fitted for my hand splints. I told the therapist I did not want to go to a formal dinner with my husband, Stephen, and use my hand splints, thinking they would stare at me. She asked whether I would want them to stare at me if I was being fed by him. She had a great point and won. I went out for the first time using my hand splints, and the stares didn't bother me.

Since then, I learned that a smile goes a long way! One of the therapists who designed my initial hand splints, Richard, reappeared in my life twenty-seven years later and was currently servicing my new hand splints. These hand splints are unusual in that they are designed to be operated by wrist movement. They are made with metal and straps of Velcro with different connections which open your finger movement from smaller to larger increments. It's a very specialized field and, therefore, costly to the patient. My first set cost $1,500 each. My second set was $1,800 each. I was left handed before my accident; however, following my accident, I became ambidextrous (needing a hand splint to write with my left hand and another to eat and put my makeup on with the right hand). It was also with the occupational therapist who taught me to drive using hand controls. I thought it would be scary driving again, but just like riding a bike, I jumped right in and adjusted to this new way to drive.

Respiratory therapy was my weakest point in the recovery. The lung is a muscle, and it was damaged during my accident along with any muscle that was below C-6-7. I probably only had 30 percent of my lung capacity operating after the accident. The purpose of the Respiratory Department was to improve this capacity and build back up the strength in my lungs. My memory of time spent here was the therapists yelling, "Blow, blow, blow!" We (about four to five patients in the room at a time) would be breathing into an apparatus, a spirometer, which measured the amount of air that you can inhale and exhale out of the lungs. A spirometer measures "forced expiratory volume," the amount of air that can be blown out of the lungs in a single second. Spirometers also measure "forced vital capacity," the total amount of air a patient can expel from his lungs. These two measurements are then used to determine the total amount of air a patient can blow out in one breath. Although my lungs have improved over the years, it is a continual problem if I get a cold or suffer from increased fluids from allergies (settling in my lungs when I'm lying down).

Behavioral medicine (BM)—the first time I saw these letters on my schedule for rehab, I could only think of a few words that fit these initials—bowel movement or maybe Bloody Mary (which would have been welcome), Baylor medicine, or bedtime movies;

and I couldn't imagine this being one of my therapies! My therapist for behavioral medicine was Melissa, a beautiful redhead with expressive eyes and a wonderful smile. We hit it off immediately. The most significant discussion I can recall was my fear of Stephen leaving me for a woman who could walk. Melissa put this in perspective with her response, "And there are a lot of walking women out there!" It made me realize that it was foolish to worry about something out of my control.

The rehab facility is just like any place where people are together over time. Rumors spread from gossip. One interesting tidbit was that I had been seen crying because the doctor told me I would never be able to have children. However, the doctor said we should wait five years to allow time for my body to heal. Paralysis doesn't generally affect a woman's ability to carry a child, especially when the nerve damage was incomplete as my injury. This is a term they use in rehabilitation for spinal cord injuries where only some of the nerves are killed or impaired. The one danger I was informed about in the delivery of a child was autonomic dysreflexia[4]—where there can be a sharp rise in blood pressure, a severe escalation or drop in heart rate, and a risk of convulsions and enlargement of the heart.

I can't leave the discussion about my rehabilitation without mentioning the nurses who took care of me, and after spending five months with them, they practically qualified as family. They were vital to my recovery and probably don't get near the credit that the therapists do. My personal care was another process I had to relearn. It was a whole new ball game! This would be from the time I wake up to going back to bed at night. The hardest part of my paralysis is the fact I must wait on someone to get me out of bed in the morning.

I was not very patient, which would add to the frustration of waiting on the nursing staff to make their rounds, take patients' vital signs and distribute medications, before we could rise for our therapy sessions each day. One of my favorite nurses was Gwen, a fellow Texas A&M Aggie, so we hit it off right away. I'm always drawn to people with a sense of humor, and I needed it more than ever! Gwen didn't treat me as an invalid. She made it fun with her crazy stories and news from the outside world.

I believe it takes a special type of person to go into the nursing field. I know there are always exceptions, as when a grouchy patient causes a nurse to have a bad day, but I found the nurses caring and competent. Gwen was not afraid to tease and make fun with me. I believe many people are afraid of how patients will react when a tragedy occurs. Although some may become bitter and not able to cope with the new lifestyle, I decided to take each day with a positive attitude, and a sense of humor always helped me along the way. There was also the dilemma of whether I should sit back and wait for a cure for paralysis or move on and adjust to what I had to work with. I chose the latter and don't regret it. As each day passed, I grew stronger and able to tackle simple tasks. I just had to learn to do things differently. One of the first tasks I conquered with my hand splint was applying my makeup. It is still the first activity performed after my caregiver leaves.

My life lesson 5: The familiar adage is true.
If you don't use it, you lose it.

FAMILY MATTERS

What is a sister?

> She is your mirror shining back at you with a
> world of possibilities.
> She is your witness who sees you at your worst
> and best,
> and loves you anyway.
> She is your partner in crime, your midnight com-
> panion, someone who
> knows when you are smiling, even in the dark.
> She is your teacher, your defense
> attorney, your personal press agent, even your
> shrink.
> Some days, she's the reason you wish you were an
> only child.
>
> —Barbara Alpert

Flashback to 1997

I presented this poem to my sister, Karen, on her birthday in a picture frame, along with a picture of us in grade school and one taken at my twentieth high school reunion. She was a year behind me in school, but this year, our classes did a joint reunion with three classes. Although I have two sisters, Karen and I were only two years apart in age and spent the most time together. We were always known as "the Little Girls," or simply "the Girls." So we were lumped together as one.

We could turn from adversaries to allies in a New York minute. One time, we said, "Shut up," to each other, which was forbidden in our household. Our punishment was having our mouths washed out with soap. We immediately went together and looked for ways to get the soap out. I believe by then we were giggling and wiping our mouths on the bedspread. My mother would find ways to "get us out of her hair" when we were fighting and complaining about the other. One time, she told us to go and write down our grievances, and once again, she heard us giggling in the bedroom, obviously not sure about this new tactic of hers.

Cherie and Karen, elementary age at house on Hollygrove, Houston, Texas

Bob, Mom, Kathryn, Cherie, Karen, 1965

January 1984

When Karen came to see me for the first time after my accident, there was nervousness on both our parts. I wish I could say she just rushed into the room and we took off from where we last ended; however, it did not happen in that manner. She was not sure how much had changed on my part, and I did not know how she would react when she saw the changes in me. The mood instantly changed when she presented me with a new summer top. When she helped me try it on, we got into a fit of laughter as my arms are difficult to put into the arm holes—like putting clothes on a young baby who cannot help you—and immediately we felt the tension drain from us both, and we felt as we always had, "the Girls." She presented me with the book *The Little Engine That Could*. The story of the little train—which had never attempted the task—successfully made it up and over the insurmountable mountain to deliver the dolls and toys to the children in the valley, saying, "I think I can. I think I can." And when he gets over the mountain, he says, "I thought I could. I thought I could." Mom inscribed, "Don't ever give up! We love you so much." Kathryn wrote, "You've come so far in such a short time. We're proud of you and love you very much." Karen wrote, "Just remember you will always be my best friend and I love you dearly."

It's proven true to this day. That book will always motivate me and bring a smile to my face and is proudly displayed on the bookshelf in the den.

My older sister, Kathryn, probably would have preferred to be an only child when "the Girls" came along. Since there was such a gap in ages, we were probably more of a nuisance to her. However, as we got older, the spread in age seemed to shrink. I got to know Kathryn as a young adult when she married and settled not too far from our house in Houston. I'm sure she was apprehensive when she visited me in the rehab. It was a different type of reunion but just as satisfying when she discovered I was the same old Cherie.

My brother Bob is the oldest sibling and regarded his younger sisters as pests while growing up. However, he was usually good-natured and accepted our intrusions with patience and humor. We might get a basketball thrown at us or bopped on the head, but we loved any attention he would throw our way.

The only way I can accurately describe when Bob first came to see me in the rehab hospital would be to compare it to the movie *The Right Stuff*, when the pilots were all striding along in their flight suits. Bob had his fellow F-15 pilot friends accompany him, and they also had come straight from the airport dressed in their flight suits. The nurses were all smitten and couldn't wait to talk to me to see who my visitors had been. I was quite popular for the day. Bob left me a special token that day. He had recently experienced a hydraulic breakdown in his plane and had to resort to using alternative procedures. One of these involved a mechanism he called a skip plate, a piece of solid metal (no more than six inches long and three to four inches wide) which saved his life! He left it with me, hoping it would bring me good luck. It was a token I have held onto for many years to remind me of the blessings in my life.

Christmas 1965

Bob, Cherie, Kathryn, Karen, 2019

CHAPTER SIX

Can She Talk?

Ft. Worth, Texas, May 1984

There had been some discussion about me staying in the rehab for another month, but I resisted because I felt I needed to go ahead and make that proverbial leap into the real world. I admit I had mixed emotions. I was both excited and frightened to leave the rehabilitation facility in May of 1984. Believe it or not, I felt safe at the rehab hospital and was frightened at the thought of not being around these trained professionals if anything went wrong. Although they spent many hours preparing Stephen on my future needs, it was still an uncertain future.

Stephen had searched for a house with accessibility and found one which required very few conversions, namely a ramp in the garage and the bathroom, which needed a roll-in shower. My sister, Karen, and her husband, Tom, (both architects) oversaw renovating the bathroom. I believe Stephen and his dad built the ramp. I was fortunate to have in-house talent which addressed my needs. But for several months after rehab, we had to live in our two-story townhome until the remodeling was complete. Before the accident, Stephen and I shared the upstairs bedroom. Upon my return, we used the room downstairs, which was not as large or as comfortable but would have to do. My sister-in-law, Jo Ella, and her son, Clay, who was three years of age, were our first visitors. Jo Ella is both mechanical and creative and has been tremendous help with repairing hand splints and wheelchair bags. While Jo Ella was inside, entertaining me with her unique perspective on some of my new equipment, Clay was outside with his uncle Stephen. Stephen was not paying attention, and Clay got behind the wheel and put the car in reverse. As it started rolling back, the passenger door was ripped off the hinges. There are few teenagers who can say they began driving at the age of three!

I remember move-in day. It would be great to have access to the whole house and not have to face so many obstacles as I had in the townhome. I felt like a kid at a candy store with everything delightful in front of me. My family was there to move everything from our two-story townhome to the house. My mother was careful to show me where things were stored since I could not help in the process. One hard thing I would have to get used to was watching things get done. It is not in my nature to sit back and let others do the job. I have learned the art of supervision.

Our daily routine would always begin early (4:00 a.m. to 5:00 a.m.). Stephen would have to stretch my muscles, perform any personal bodily functions, and shower before dressing for the day. We showered together for expediency's sake. Once he helped me with my clothes and got me into my power wheelchair for the day, he could take care himself. I could help with buttoning my blouses with a specialized tool they sent me home with; although, it was often faster for Stephen to do it. Once I was in the wheelchair, I could blow dry my hair and apply my own makeup. He then would prepare our breakfast and then be off for the day. Stephen continued to be my caregiver throughout the marriage. In hindsight, we probably should have hired a service. It did not seem to hinder the relationship through many of our years together; however, as time went on, it must have bothered him more than he was willing to admit. Although I can't turn back the clock, this was a change I would have made.

Amazing as it may seem, I was back at work at Carter Blood Center by August 1984, only nine months from the time of the accident and three months from my rehabilitation. My occupational therapist stated this was extremely rare to get back to work so quickly after a debilitating accident of my nature. The Rehabilitation Commission had committed to financing the cost of my hand controls and wheelchair lift in a Ford Econoline that Stephen had purchased for my transportation. This is the most independent feeling a person with a disability can experience, not depending upon someone else for transportation. Unfortunately, it would take nine months to complete the whole process from authorization to receiving the renovated van.

In the interim nine months, I rode the public transportation called MITS (Mobility Impaired Transportation Service) to and from work. That was an enlightening experience of its own. As before in rehabilitation, I compared myself to others and saw how blessed I was. The same held true here. I rode together with people of varying degrees of disabilities from mild to severe in form. One who comes to mind was a young man with Tourette's syndrome. He would express himself with colorful curse words from the time we left my house until we arrived at Carter Blood Center where I worked. I resumed work as the community relations director, where my responsibilities included writing, editing, and publishing the quarterly newsletter; media relations with local newspapers and television stations; and employee recognition programs. I was fortunate in that my immediate boss, Richard Wilson, believed in me from the time of the accident. He had come to see me in the hospital and said that my job would be waiting for me when I returned. I believe he suffered much grief from the general manager over the years I worked there for making this commitment, but he stood by me, nevertheless. It also gave me a goal to work toward as I was going through my rehabilitation. For this, I will always be grateful to him.

I worked seven years at Carter Blood Center and cherished the people I worked with. One person who sticks out in my mind was Bill, an older gentleman who was puzzled by my situation. I believe he was probably shocked when I returned to work and was interested in everything with my condition. In one specific instance, I had fallen from my wheelchair and was yelling for help from my office. The door was unfortunately closed, so I had to yell loud as my voice did not carry very far. Bill happened to walk by and heard me and immediately got help to lift me back in the wheelchair. I probably fell at least two more times while I worked there. I would relieve pressure from my bottom by leaning forward while holding onto straps hooked to each side of the wheelchair. One side would invariably break and would cause me to shift to that side, and the momentum would cause me to keep rolling in that direction and ultimately to the floor. The first time, I cried from embarrassment. The remaining few times, I would laugh at myself and share my folly with others. My best memory of Bill was when I announced I was pregnant, and the expression on his face was priceless of "How did that happen?" I still think he remained puzzled about me until he died shortly before I left the blood center.

The three individuals who kept me sane and appreciated my humor and treated me as "normal" were Larry, Eileen, and Maggie. We had many laughs together. One included creating a program for our annual Christmas party. We spent weeks working on the poem from Dr. Seuss's story *The Day the Grinch Stole Christmas*. Our version was *The Day the Grinch Stole the Christmas Blood Drive*! We even created a slideshow with fun pictures of the staff and associating it with the blood shortage during the holidays.

The early '80s was a challenging time for the Blood Center, when the AIDS crisis first exploded. As community relations director, it was my job to ensure the public that the blood supply was tested and would not pass on the AIDS virus. I would never forget trying to convince an older gentleman, probably in his seventies, that you could not get AIDS from donating blood, regardless of how Rock Hudson got it! I turned out to be one of those needing blood the previous year. I required one pint during my spinal cord surgery. Interestingly, I did not worry about that pint I was given until I became pregnant five years later and needed a blood test. The three or four days I waited were filled with fear and nervousness. Fortunately, the blood supply and pint given to me was perfectly safe.

Another fun memory of Eileen and Maggie was when I showed up at work with blood all down the front of my skirt. Stephen had shaved my legs that morning and had accidentally cut my knee with the razor. Apparently, neither of us was aware of it at the time or before I left for work. When I arrived at work, Eileen saw it and exclaimed, "Your leg!" and ran off to get first aid items. Maggie yelled, "Your dress!" and ran to get saline solution, which I discovered is great for removing bloodstains. Both instances fit their personalities, and I love them both for all they did for me while we worked together.

Larry was with me one time in the grocery store to buy an item for work. While we waited to be checked out, the cashier looked at me and asked Larry, "Can she talk?" I wish I could remember his clever response, because out of the group, he was by far the most outrageous. I know we had many fine laughs from that story. The first time I was told, "I don't see the wheelchair," was by these friends. I was riding with Eileen, and we were going to pick up Larry (his car had broken down). As we were pulling up, Eileen said, "Stop here!" It was on the opposite side of my lift where I could not get out. She said, "I forget you're in the wheelchair." This has always been the greatest compliment, and I often hear it from those who know me well.

When I first started working for Carter Blood Center, I was hired as a donor recruiter, a representative who went out to local businesses and organizations to "recruit" blood donors. It was understood that as soon as the community involvement position came available, I would slide into that role. It was to my advantage that the position of community relations director was created after my accident; otherwise, I might not have been able to continue working there. As donor recruiter, you were required to take audiovisual equipment out to make presentations to various groups. This obviously would have been impossible to perform on my own merit; I believe fate had a helping hand here!

My life lesson 6: Friends are angels in disguise.

CHAPTER SEVEN

Helpless but Not Hopeless

House on Morely Avenue, Ft. Worth, June 1984

On the home front, I was working with two therapists as an outpatient. My physical therapist, Glen, would come several times a week to help me learn to maneuver from my wheelchair to my bed and back or transferring to a car. To say I was helpless was an understatement. I believe Glen worked with me over a year, and I could never master the task independently. I have short arms compared to my legs and could never get my arms underneath the legs to lift them on to the bed. I remember stating that I was klutzy when I was walking. Glen assured me, "Once a klutz, always a klutz!" We had a great time trying to get it right. I always appreciate a good sense of humor with any given situation. If you could give me a grade upon completion, it would be a B–. I could assist with my upper body in sliding over on a smooth wooden board to get into bed, onto a shower chair, in a car, etc. The nice aspect for my care givers was they did not have to lift my deadweight (lower body) without any assistance. I weighed about 130, but it probably felt like 200 without me helping!

My other therapist was Kathy, an occupational therapist, who tried to help me function in the kitchen. One thing important to mention about my experience in the kitchen is before my accident, I was a novice. I was just beginning to experiment with cooking in the early months of my marriage. The only meal I had successfully prepared was the one I made for Stephen when he proposed—Cornish game hens and potatoes. I once invited a couple to dinner with Stephen and myself with this same menu. The dessert I decided to try was a favorite of Stephen's, and I had gotten the recipe from his mom. Unfortunately, I did not read the recipe all the way through before beginning. I realized I had made a mistake when at the end of the recipe, it read, "Add remaining sugar." The crust came out hard as a rock! Everyone had a good laugh from it, but I learned cooking was going to be a challenge. Just the task of opening cans and getting prepared to cook became a challenge. Kathy could see my reluctance and could see she was working with a losing cause. Truth be told, I let Stephen take over this task. I had no problem becoming a princess here.

Kathy worked with me when my new van was delivered and went out with me on my maiden voyage. I had learned to drive with hand controls in a car at the rehab facility. Kathy had driven me to the parking lot of the Cowboys stadium in Dallas. Initially, I was frightened to get behind the wheel after my accident, but once the car started moving, it felt powerful to overcome my fears. The hand controls consist of a bar on the left which is used for both acceleration and braking. I push down to accelerate and push forward to brake. For steering, my wrist fits between three posts protruding from the steering wheel. Every conversion is specific to the individual. It felt entirely different driving from my wheelchair. I felt uneasy with my precarious balance—particularly with left turns. Kathy held my shoulders from behind at the beginning; however, it does not need to be pointed out that I could not continue with Kathy at my shoulder or making only right turns for the rest of my life. I did finally become comfortable; however, to this day, I still don't make a left-hand turn without careful consideration.

I love the independent feeling of having my own vehicle. I appreciate this perhaps the most. It allows me the freedom to get to work, go shopping, and visit friends. I appreciate it even more when my van breaks down and I must rely on public transportation.

Kathy also encouraged me to attempt swimming. My boss graciously allowed us to come over to use his pool. I was an excellent swimmer in my elementary school years. My parents were members of a country club, where I discovered the love of swimming when a lifeguard observed my ability and encouraged me to join the swim team. He was my first crush on an older boy. My cat, Dudley, was named after him. I went on to win first place trophies and ribbons in freestyle, backstroke, and the butterfly. The only swim stroke I struggled with was the breaststroke. After my injury, I was no longer comfortable when Stephen tried to get me back into the pool to enjoy the benefits of water therapy. I did not like the feeling when my face would slip below the water surface, and I would come up choking on water. I was disappointed I could not swim like a fish as my friend, Natalie, could.

My life lesson 7: Always have a plan B!

CHAPTER EIGHT

Things Even a Quad Should Avoid

Mud: Just as a car should avoid mud, so should anyone in a wheelchair. I forgot this concept one day. I'm not sure what was so important to get to the fence at our yard. However, in the process, I got so bogged down I couldn't move until Stephen came along and pulled me out.

Ice: I believe it was on one of the first mornings of ice on the streets in Ft. Worth when I had begun driving on my own. I was heading down to my van and lost control of my wheelchair. Once again, I forgot I'm like a small car and can spin out just the same!

Sand: Our first real vacation from the time of the accident was to Long Beach, California, to visit my good friend and college roommate, Yvette and her husband, Clay. We could not just pack and go like most folks do on a trip. There were so many more things to consider for my medical needs. Just getting on an airplane was a big project. Stephen always did all the lifting to and from the plane seat. But in the end, it was worth the trouble. We visited Universal Studios and had a blast mimicking the Rolling Stones on a video. I was the drummer who couldn't hold on to my drumsticks! When we went out to the beach one afternoon, we realized wheelchairs do not roll through sand, so Stephen carried the wheelchair out to the beach first and then came back and carried me out to the wheelchair. I lasted all but fifteen minutes before I couldn't handle the cool temperature and asked to leave. I know I was being a pain, but back then my temperature control in my body did not work well. My body was like an older person. I used to stay covered in blankets during the winters in Ft. Worth. I do not know if it came from gaining weight or because my body had acclimated, but I do not feel so vulnerable in the cold temperatures anymore.

My life lesson 8: Learn to laugh at yourself.

CHAPTER NINE

A New Mode for Exercise

Ft. Worth, 1997

After little success in pushing my manual wheelchair around a track for exercise in a slow but persistent forty-minute mile, I was chosen to participate in an exercise program. It combined functional electrical stimulation (electrodes placed on my legs at key points where the nerve impulse fires and the muscle contracts) with computer technology to control muscle contractions of paralyzed legs. It also would increase blood circulation and muscle tone as well as improve my cardiovascular system. The research was designed to determine the changes and/or benefits to the muscle fiber resulting from the exercise program.

I drove into the afternoon sun to Dallas three times per week for therapy, which is approximately forty miles one way. I then realized what it was like for Stephen when he visited me practically every day for five months while I was in Dallas Rehabilitation. The insurance company eventually approved a bike of my own which cost $18,000! Believe it or not, I still had money left under the policy from my accident when I thought that it would be gone after five months of rehabilitation. The bike exercise was a slow process and extremely frustrating as my legs would fatigue quickly and shut down the computer program. The way the program worked was Stephen would have to initially rotate my legs during a two-minute warm-up and let go when the computer took over, and my legs would work on their own with the assistance of the electrodes. This would optimally last twenty minutes; however, my legs would fatigue within five minutes, and the program would shift to the cool-down mode where

Stephen would have to assist again. We would get up in the early hours, when I would be less likely to fatigue; spend fifteen minutes applying the electrodes; transfer on to the bike (which was approximately six to seven feet long and weighed a ton); exercise for ten to fifteen minutes, depending on my energy that morning; and spend another fifteen minutes transferring back to my wheelchair, getting the electrodes back off. We both still had a full day at work ahead of us! By the time, I was finally able to make it the full twenty minutes in October of 1988, I discovered I was pregnant with Carissa and stopped the exercise. I did not know the ramifications during pregnancy and would not take any chances.

In his "nesting" mode, Stephen decided to make some home improvements. He removed the flooring in the kitchen and carpet in the den and replaced it with parquet tile. I had several misgivings and was terrified of inhaling the fumes during the process. I remember staying in our bedroom with the covers over my head due to being pregnant and not wanting to harm the baby!

In March, we went to Houston for Stephen's outpatient radial keratotomy[5] surgery to correct his nearsightedness. It was a combination business trip and vacation while he recovered from surgery on both eyes. Following the surgery, it must have been interesting for the eye clinic personnel to observe him being led out and driven home by a pregnant paralyzed woman in a wheelchair!

In June of 1987, I was flattered to have a letter I had written to Norman Vincent Peale published in one of his inspiring magazines called *Plus*. The letter focused on the faith I had gained from the car accident. I wrote,

> From the time of the accident up to this very day, I have been learning what faith is about. I was very close to death following the accident, but I never lost faith that God was there by my side and I would be given a second chance. I can recall talking out loud to God and letting him know I still felt a purpose in life and would not give up. At that point I had no idea what

43

lay ahead. I just knew I wanted to live. My faith in my marriage as well as my faith in God was greatly strengthened at this time. Stephen and I had only been married six months when the accident occurred. Many people were surprised that he stuck by my side since others in similar circumstances do not have the strength to cope with such a burden. I just thank God for His influence in my life and that my faith in Him has given me the opportunity to grow spiritually, to keep on growing and to share my faith with others.

I received much more out of writing the letter than just seeing my name in print. A woman from Oklahoma became my pen pal for a short time as a result. It was rewarding to know my story helped another person.

My life lesson 9: From Proverbs 16:9, "In his heart a man plans his course, but the Lord determines his steps."

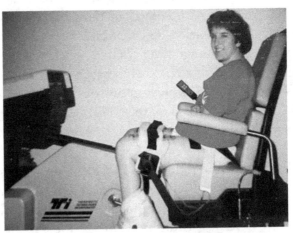

Functional Stimulation Bike

CHILDHOOD

I believe my childhood was idyllic. I grew up in a middle-class neighborhood with loving parents and siblings. Our neighborhood had many kids around my age, and we would spend hours playing together until we were called in by our parents. My mother was known for her distinctive clapping to call us in. We had little hope of staying out past 10:00 p.m. because back in those days, a message came across the television, "It's 10:00 p.m. Do you know where your children are?" We would not be far but would have to end our activities once we heard her clap. We had a huge open field behind our house for years when I was young in a neighborhood which backed up to Hobby Airport. We would spend hours creating what we termed "bird nests" or forts. We didn't spend our afternoons and evenings in front of a television, and it was before computer games, so we would let our imaginations take us away to fun places. I was always an active child. I loved to run from an early age and would either run or ride my bike to friends' houses, to the park, and to the 7-Eleven. I am amazed when I think of how far I could go, and my mother did not have a cell phone to track me down!

When I was in the sixth grade, my father decided he wanted to invest in land outside Houston. He had talked it over with my mom. I learned later in life, he made an "executive" decision to purchase a hundred acres between Anderson and Navasota—off Highway 6 between Hempstead and College Station, Texas. My childhood became even more idyllic because we would spend the week in the city and most weekends in the country. As time passed, my father started dabbling in ranch work. He started with two Charolais cows which originated from Charolles, France. He named our ranch "Trois Eperon," which means "three spurs" in English. I remember being terribly excited

45

when the female cow Chloe was to give birth to "our" first calf. I tried sleeping out beside her, thinking I would catch all the excitement. I learned that, on the contrary, she would not have spectators.

Overall, the ranch brings back wonderful memories of building trails through the woods, swimming in the ponds on the property, swinging on vines across the creeks, and sharing special conversations and moments with my family. We also developed great friendships with the local residents and even went on daylong trail rides when the opportunity arose. A local favorite was a dance hall called the Moose. This was where I learned to country dance. What most people remember about our place (both the locals and friends we invited from Houston) was our pond. One of my friends, Kevin, from school called our float in the middle of the pond the "Big Aspirin." It was part of a water aeration system my dad had gotten from a customer and did, in fact, resemble a giant aspirin floating on the water. It gave us hours of entertainment since it would spin as we ran on top of the Big Aspirin in circles in one direction and then switch directions, and we would have contests to see who could stay on longest.

Before the accident, I was an early riser and ready to run a mile, if time permitted. I ran track in high school. As I remember back then, there were not many competitors in the 1,600 meters (four times around the track), so I was often racing against the clock or against my best previous times at that distance. Karen liked to recall the half marathon we ran together while in college at Texas A&M. It was the first time for both of us to attempt this goal, and I left a lasting impression with Karen when I threw up my fluids as I crossed the finish line.

I was running five miles per day at the time of the accident, and my tennis shoes showed the wear and tear. I teased the staff and said I was faking it and secretly running around the building at night. I come from a family of Aggies. My uncle Jerry Bonnen was the original and first "Fightingest Texas Aggie," for his extreme effort—collapsing over the finish line on to his knees for fourth place. This motivated the Aggies team following his race to go on to beat the University of Texas, their archrivals, for the conference championship.

Stubbornness runs in my blood. We all have hard heads. My grandfather Dixon fell down a twenty-five-to-thirty-foot embankment while trying to lay some stones for steps down to the creek bed. It's a miracle he didn't suffer any trauma or even drown from the incident. Likewise, I was riding a horse bareback when I was a teenager and flipped over its head and landed flat on my back when the horse stopped suddenly. I was told to use a saddle for safety but stubbornly ignored this advice. I remember my dad running out from the back door of the house and my mother sprinting out from the front door to check on my condition. I was a little stunned, but no physical injuries were evident. It's amazing I did not break my neck on that day. The same stubbornness helps me do things with my disability. In other words, I don't give up easily when attempting something on my own. Sure, if someone is there with me, I'll accept the help. However, if I'm alone, I'll persevere.

Stubbornness can also come in the form of not recognizing health issues. I share this with my father because I would delay recognizing symptoms when I didn't want to go to the doctor or hospital.

My father died suddenly of a heart attack, three months before he would turn fifty-five years old. To say it devastated my family is an understatement. It was such a shock since he didn't appear to have any health problems. We later discovered he was taking antacid tablets, which masks the problem at hand. A person might think he has indigestion, and more serious problems could be the case. He apparently was holding more stress internally than we were aware of.

My dad was a chemical engineer who loved learning and then teaching those interested. He was patient with me with most things, but one of my fond memories of him while I was in college was when I had to take my first chemistry class (which was like a foreign language to me). When he was trying to help me one day and I was not catching on to the concept, he exclaimed, "I don't understand why you don't understand this!" My mother simply said, "She's not a chemical engineer, honey."

My favorite times with him were when he liked to explain how things worked or about the cattle. He only lost his patience with me when it came to my finances. I was never good at reconciling my checkbook and would overdraw the account frequently. He was going over it with me one evening and got to a rather large overdraft and simply threw the checkbook up in the air. Despite this, he came to me later and discussed a budget I should follow.

My mother was the strongest woman I knew, and I truly give her credit for my positive attitude. After all, she was one who has had challenges but remained positive and strong in her faith despite it all. This began with the death of her third child, my brother Richard Clay Dixon. He died from a brain tumor at the precious age of three. Following his death, when I was about six months, my mother grew concerned from my lack of activity and inability to walk (compared to her previous experience with my brother and sister), so she took me in for a routine checkup. She was informed a short time later, rather insensitively, on the phone that my bones had fused and I would either be a dwarf, or, if not treated, possibly even die. My parents didn't accept this diagnosis and sought a second opinion from the doctor who had helped them with Richard's care. Dr. Erickson fortunately had some knowledge about bone growth and discovered that I suffered from hypothyroidism.[6] He x-rayed my arm and discovered a "floating" bone, which meant that there was still a possibility for future bone growth. In fact, once I started taking medication for my thyroid, I grew eight inches in a year. During this difficult time, she also learned she was pregnant with my younger sister, Karen. Later in life when she went through the experience of witnessing my father's heart attack, she once again demonstrated strength and maintained her faith in God.

The day my dad died, he and my mom were out doing what my dad loved, planting grass. One moment he was walking along planting, the next moment he was down on the ground lifeless! My mother tried CPR; however, the damage to his heart was so severe; we believe he died immediately. I can't imagine how my mom coped out there alone, without help. It probably seemed a lifetime before somebody drove by and could help her. Once again, she proved how strong she was. My dad had always taken care of her in every way. She learned how to handle her own finances and from then on practically took care of the ranch on her own into her eighties. Many years later, my brother commented he couldn't believe how this one woman took care of so many things on the property.

My mom was a great role model. I grew up watching her strength, so when it came time for me to show mine, I knew exactly what I needed to do.

Karen, my dad, me, and Mom at a wedding, Anderson, Texas, 1976

My mom and me at my wedding, July 9, 1983

Karen and Cherie, half-marathon participants

CHAPTER TEN

We Did It the Old-Fashioned Way

Ft. Worth, June 1989

When I became pregnant[7] with my first child, Carissa, there were various reactions. As I mentioned previously, one was Bill's reaction of "How?" My favorite had to be "How beautifully bold of them!" I had the pleasure of "sitting in" as Karen's matron of honor at her wedding in October of 1988. It was there we started suspecting I was pregnant. Sure enough, after I returned from the weekend of festivities, my blood test confirmed it. I realize women should not announce they are pregnant until after the first trimester; however, I was on "cloud nine" and couldn't help myself! I told everyone who crossed my path. I would have found a way to slip it in on a television interview if there had been a blood shortage at the time! Both of our families were supportive of our decision to start a family. Despite the risks involved, we knew we wanted children. There were doubts as to whether I could manage the necessary tasks to take care of children, especially as infants, but we were both determined to face those challenges. One of my fears was how my children would feel about a disabled mom as adolescents. I was blessed my daughters never felt embarrassed or ashamed having a mom in a wheelchair.

Circumstances were the same for me as it is for any able-bodied pregnant woman. I had bouts of morning sickness, but nothing dreadful or long-lasting. I enjoyed shopping for maternity clothing when I started expanding. I could not wait for this occurrence! However, risks included increased bladder infections, which became problematic if antibiotics were introduced; pressure sores due to the weight gain; autonomic dysreflexia; and hypertension. One issue that concerned me was the medication I was on for spasms (Baclofen) and whether it would affect my unborn child. There were not many quadriplegics having babies back then. By happenstance, there was a local article on a young woman with a spinal cord injury who had given birth that year. I immediately called her and asked if I could speak to her about her pregnancy, as I was in the same situation. She agreed and revealed not only had she been on Baclofen, but she had also been on birth control pills through five months of her pregnancy! I wasn't so worried after that.

My next scare came when a test came back positive which indicated our child could possibly be born with spina bifida. My first thought was Stephen had more than he could handle with just my needs. What would this do to our already-stressful lives? There was no thought to terminating even if this had occurred; however, after praying and crying for three days, the more extensive sonogram showed no signs of spina bifida. I was told false-positive results happen often with these blood tests. I was so relieved! We were back to a one-wheelchair household and could go on planning for a healthy newborn in June.

Another consideration was the question of knowing how I would know it was time to go to the hospital when I went into labor. I don't remember who put me in touch with the group, but I was monitored twenty-four hours a day, seven days a week starting around my eighth month. If the apparatus I wore around my waist detected anything remotely resembling a contraction, I would be contacted and must drink water to determine if the contraction was real or not. I'm not sure what the significance of drinking water meant concerning contractions. I remember having many false contractions and got tired of the process by the time my ninth month rolled around. When I went into labor, it wasn't the monitoring apparatus that determined my going in. It was the fact my water broke while in bed early morning. When I felt the uncomfortable feeling of being soaked, I woke Stephen up to tell him we needed to go to the hospital. He thought we could just wait, as I had a scheduled appointment with the nurse in the morning. In hindsight, he was probably correct, but I wasn't taking any chances. He loaded me in the car. Transferring me on a regular basis was always a challenge. Can you imagine what me with twenty more pounds in my midsection must have been like? We hurried to Harris Hospital around 4:00 a.m. I got admitted and waited for the excitement to begin. It was boring waiting during labor. I did not have to blow, and Stephen did not have to act as my coach, helping me relax during contractions.

Paralysis does not generally affect a woman's ability to carry a child, especially when the nerve damage is incomplete as mine was. This is a term they use in rehabilitation for spinal cord injuries where only some of the nerves are killed or impaired. The one danger I was informed about in the delivery of a child was autonomic dysreflexia. That is where there could be a sharp rise in blood pressure, a severe escalation or lowering heart rate, and a risk of convulsions and enlargement of the heart.

I was not happy to discover my doctor was on vacation and would not be delivering my baby. Here was this quadriplegic woman with very specific issues with her delivery, and he didn't feel the need to be there! I was not even told he would be on vacation during the week of my due date. So I had the doctor on call, who didn't know anything about my situation, and approached it as he would any "normal" delivery. Once the doctor felt I was close, he gave me Pitocin, which stimulates the contractions. Pitocin is prescribed for causing or improving uterine contractions in pregnant women. I took it to minimize complications and to help the doctor mimic normal labor as much as possible. One thing that was not in the delivery room was a blood pressure cuff, or if there was, my blood pressure wasn't being monitored constantly as it should have been. One of the risks I was warned about prior to having a child was the danger of high blood pressure causing a stroke during the delivery. I began having a severe headache during Carissa's delivery and felt sure this was happening. I was frightened in the delivery room when Carissa was born since they did not monitor my blood pressure even during this time.

I was scared and had to be given something for the pain before I could hold my new baby daughter for the first time. It didn't take long for those big blue eyes to eliminate any thought of the stroke I thought I was having. She was worth the danger.

The big event occurred right on schedule. Carissa was due on June 13, 1989, and was born on Flag Day, June 14, 1989, at 2:38 p.m. She came after fourteen hours of labor, if you could call it that. She arrived during one of my favorite soap operas, *The Guiding Light*. Until the Pitocin kicked in and began the dilation process, Stephen had been lounging close by while I watched my CBS soap operas. Many would assume that Carissa was born Caesarean. However, she came vaginally with no complications and little effort on my part. I can't begin to describe how nervous I was to be responsible for this newborn. How would I hold her without dropping her? How would I change her diapers? The tasks seemed daunting for this mom, who, despite her independence once out of the bed, could not imagine what it would be to take care of a baby totally dependent upon me. I admit that it would be a couple of months before I felt comfortable changing her diaper on my own. I learned to pull the tabs on and off with my teeth (not pleasant task when removing dirty diapers). Fortunately, both our parents came to help, first my mom, waving a small American flag (as it was Flag Day), and then within two weeks, Stephen's parents.

I was given the usual six-week maternity leave from work. We began immediately searching for a caregiver to help with Carissa's care. I did not feel comfortable staying home alone with her because I would need help with feeding and diapering Carissa. I would place her upon a pillow on my lap to breastfeed with help from Sybil, the extraordinary woman we found to care for Carissa. She was from Sierra Leon, Africa, and more loving and good-natured than I could ever hope to find in a helper. It was a rough six weeks for me physically, but being stubborn and hard-headed helped me survive the challenging hormonal imbalance. Once I started back to work on July 27, our schedule was bordering on normalcy. We would wake up around 4:00 a.m. Stephen would help me set up to pump my breasts for breast milk to feed her while I was at work, and he would doze until it was time to change to the next breast. We would then get up to start our showering and dressing routine. I can't believe that we kept up with this routine for a year.

My life lesson 10: I have always enjoyed the song, "Anything you can do, I can do better!" for determination.

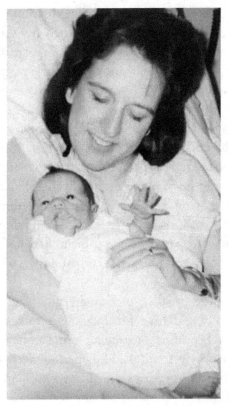

Cherie with Carissa, 1989

CHAPTER ELEVEN

The Quad Way to Do It

Ft. Worth, 1990–1991

I was much like most new mothers, apprehensive and nervous; but instead of dwelling on things I could not accomplish or the way other mothers do it, I figured how to make it work. This ability to adapt was what set my family apart. As Carissa got a little bigger, I became more adept at handling her basic needs, such as feeding, diapering, getting her out of the crib and onto my lap. She even chuckled when she has done a headstand in the process! She was always patient, as if she understood I was different from most mothers. Not many mothers have to diaper with their teeth! She has always had a matter-of-fact attitude about my disability. My wheelchair was her chariot! She loved riding on my lap, even if it was just across the house. She loved picking up things I dropped, a recurring incidence throughout my life. What is most inspiring is the way she adjusted to getting in my lap. She learned early on, as soon as she could climb (see Carissa's essay "I Climbed Before I Crawled"). Many times, I'm sure she wondered if I would succeed in getting her from point A to point B. I can't deny the question I saw in her eye. But more important was the trust and faith, which made me try much harder. Carissa experienced all the usual developmental tasks at the age the books said she would; however, she had developed her own personal character resulting from her environment. For instance, she knew to look out when Mom was driving through the room in her wheelchair—especially if I backed up! She inherited her Mimi Dixon's (my mom) compulsion for order—always putting her toys back where they belong. She realized that toys left out may get run over. Once, I even rolled over her ball and popped it. When we took her to the store to buy a new one, she picked out the largest ball she could find, I believe thinking her mom could not roll over one so large!

Carissa watched everything Stephen did for me and seemed to understand that I needed assistance on daily tasks. I could see her joining a union by age three! However, she appreciated being a child first, then a helper. She did mimic me in many of the ways I dressed her. One of these tasks was putting on her socks. I would pull her socks on to her feet with my teeth. So the next thing I saw was Carissa trying to pull her socks on with her own teeth! I corrected her and said this is the "quad way to do it."

I often find myself in absurd situations I never would have before my accident. My first van had a wheelchair lift which lifted from the ground and would swing in at the top to drop me down on the van floor. As I rose that morning on the lift with the weather in the thirties, I came to the top to swing in, but the mechanism stopped and would not swing in, nor would it go back down to the ground. I was stuck at the top! I was dressed warmly; however, large overcoats on me were out of the question as it would be too bulky to drive in. I was freezing! We lived on the frontage road of I-20, so with all the noise from the freeway, it would be a miracle if Sybil could ever hear me yelling from outside. I knew she probably had the television on by then as well. This was also before cell phones were commonplace. I believe one of my angels must have been watching over me that day and gave Sybil a signal I needed help. She came out and saw my predicament, brought me a large blanket to cover my cold body, and called Stephen to come back home to help. I know I must have been a sight from the access road. It probably looked like a teepee hanging in the air beside my van. Although we had my van which I could drive independently, we bought a new car in 1990 with hand controls. This way, when we went on family trips, I could help with the driving. I'm sure Stephen had reservations about having them installed once I was behind the wheel, as I enjoyed the feeling of driving a much sportier car than a large van. We took several trips to Kansas to see Stephen's grandparents and to Chicago to see his parents. My favorite trips back then were Thanksgiving holidays with his family—even though it was a long drive, especially with an eighteen-month child.

As Carissa neared eighteen months of age, we felt, even though she benefited from this nurturing one-on-one environment, she was ready for a more structured atmosphere, complete with social and educational opportunities. She began preschool at KinderCare. Another big change also took place. I bid Carter Blood Center a fond farewell and started the New Year working in the marketing department of Fort Worth Rehabilitation Hospital (FWRH). Once Carissa had started in the day care and I began in the hospital, the germs found us in one place or the other! With my new job came new stresses, which opened the door to illness. Since my lung capacity is compromised from the spinal cord injury, my ability to fight off germs is challenging. Ironically, I almost became an inpatient within weeks of being employed with FWRH. I caught the worst respiratory infection since my injury and received respiratory therapy on an outpatient basis. Carissa didn't understand why her daddy would push on my stomach to help me get a cough out, so she would start crying and ask if "Mommy was otay." After getting used to this routine, her concerned expression was priceless as she would ask, "Bad cough?" or "Feel better now?"

At two and a half, Carissa was becoming possessive of her "mommy" and would not allow her friends at KinderCare to touch my wheelchair when I came to visit. She claimed exclusive rights on riding, her favorite spot being between my feet on the front pedals— moving my feet aside so she could fit comfortably. She also became a parrot, often repeat-ing my "You-whooing" to get Stephen's attention if I was in bed and needed him. She was also a big entertainer, using anything she could

get her hands on as a microphone. My personal favorite was the cat's tail. I found it amazing Dudley cooperated and did not scratch her.

I got a new motorized wheelchair in June of that year. You would think with a new wheelchair, there would be no problems for at least a year. Not so in my experience with medical equipment. One day at work, I discovered that my brand-new wheelchair would not drive forward! I'm sure I was a spectacle as I backed down the halls that day! Stephen showed up and transferred me to my manual wheelchair, and shortly afterward, both the tires blew out!

I know I was hysterical when I called the wheelchair serviceman to come ASAP. Even though I could laugh later, it was then I decided the name for my book was appropriate. You might start to notice that wheelchair problems are a factor I deal with routinely. It ranges anywhere from aggravating to the absurd. In 1991, Stephen said, "A sick cat, a howling dog, a screaming two-year-old and a quadriplegic wife—why would I leave all of this?" Why would he indeed?

My life lesson 11: Your differences can set you apart.

CHAPTER TWELVE

A Second Blessing Despite the Odds

Ft. Worth, 1992

When I look back over 1992, all I can remember is the ups and downs of being pregnant with our second child. I started off with a respiratory infection and developed sores on my heels due to edema. Then I discovered that I had gestational diabetes, just when I started enjoying eating for two! I think it was to punish me for buying up all the new Almond M&M's in the vending machine. My guilty conscience must have affected my blood sugar. I spent the last three months wearing big black ROJO boots with sheepskin liners to keep the pressure off my heels. ROJO boots provide an adjustable therapeutic environment which aids in the healing/prevention of heal ischemic ulcers. It minimizes friction while helping to maintain blood flow to the wound sight, controlling edema and facilitating the healing of damaged tissue. My physical therapist stated that I would see the baby before I would see regular shoes, and she was right. It was overshadowed by our excitement when we found out I would be having another girl. Carissa couldn't wait to welcome her new sister. She would often practice with a doll. I only gained five pounds, even though gestational babies are often big babies. We were worried about premature birth because she was so small this far along.

We decided to take a summer vacation before the baby was due. We drove to Phoenix, Arizona, and stayed at a resort hotel, where we relaxed and enjoyed the amenities. It seemed we could not take any trips without car problems, and this was no exception. Stephen had been gone an extremely long time to get the car repaired while I was in bed resting. At one point, I became rather worried and wept about what I would do if he didn't return. Carissa came to my side and—with the most adult, sympathetic tone—said, "You poor thing. Everything is going to be okay." She had always been sensitive but has always amazed me with her matter-of-fact attitude about my needs. When she would get upset with us, her standard response was, "I'm going to tell my baby sister on you!" Stephen fortunately returned with the car repaired several hours later.

When I went to work one morning, two weeks prior to my due date, I was experiencing chills and fever and could not seem to get comfortable no matter how many blankets were applied. I had grown close to one of the nurses at work, Deb, and respected her for her knowledge and the way she cared about each patient's individual needs. I asked her to go with me to the doctor. The nurse from the doctor's office kept asking questions, but when she got to the part about why I was wearing a jacket over my head, I know Deb was about to lose it. The nurse could not seem to grasp that I had vastly different symptoms and different needs from a routine patient. I do not feel pain as a result of my injury; however, my body will demonstrate the pain in other ways. My sweat glands do not work anymore, but when I'm experiencing pain my blood pressure rises, my skin becomes clammy, and I sweat profusely. I have learned over the years through trial and error what is causing these dysreflexia symptoms.

On October 19, 1992, I was admitted to the hospital because of a urinary infection—the bane of my existence. Once that was under control, my doctor became concerned about my anemia and how it was affecting my baby. He decided it was best to induce on Thursday, October 22. The original plan had been to induce at noon. We called my mom to give her the news, and directly following, the doctor came in and said his board meeting had been canceled and he was ready to induce at 8:30 a.m. Cailey arrived at 11:30 a.m.! The doctor didn't even make it back in time. My lovely Irish nurse, Eva, delivered her! I could hear Stephen through the wall when she was taken into be weighed, and he exclaimed excitedly, "Five pounds, nine ounces!" This was a different doctor than when I was pregnant with Carissa, and he acted genuinely disappointed in not getting back in time.

I'm sure it was not a common occurrence, and he was looking forward to the novelty of delivering a baby from a quadriplegic mother. When we called my mom back, she thought we would just be getting started when I informed her of Cailey's birth.

One story for the baby book, which we can laugh about now but was embarrassing when it happened, was when we were packing the car and leaving the hospital with Cailey. Stephen had left the driver's door open with the engine running to let the car cool while loading her in the car seat in back. Carissa, thinking she was being helpful, hit the power door lock button and shut the driver's door shut at the same time Stephen was closing the rear door where Cailey had been placed—consequently, locking Cailey in by herself! Security personnel couldn't get the door open, so fortunately the air conditioning was on, and she didn't suffer any until our next-door neighbor arrived with an extra set of keys. In fact, I believe she napped through the entire affair

My life lesson 12: When stressed, take a nap. It works for kids.

Carissa and Cailey, 1992

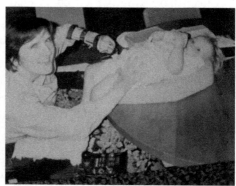
Using hand splint to diaper Cailey

CHAPTER THIRTEEN

Mommy Told Me Not to Tell You

Ft. Worth, 1993

Two significant events occurred in 1993. First, in July, we had celebrated ten years of marriage. Then in December, I had now been injured for ten years. The expression "Time flies when you're having fun" could also be "When you're busy." This was true with two children. I also had put a hundred thousand miles on my van. Who would have guessed ten years ago I would ever drive again, let alone put so many miles on my vehicle? My best therapy in the ten years has been parenting, which channeled my focus on the girls instead of my issues. It was not hard to imagine what could be accomplished when little trusting eyes looked up at you while exclaiming, "You can do it, Mommy!" I would later use this expression at Carissa's wedding in 2016.

If there was ever a child described as "four going on twenty-one," it would be Carissa. She had practically helped raise Cailey from the day she was brought home. Many kids at the age of four can handle changing diapers and help with feeding the baby, but how many do you know who could carry a baby around quite competently and lift the baby to and from the mother's lap? She even helped me get Cailey out of the car seat, even though her sister was already half her body weight. I always tried to respect Carissa's limits, though. When I had asked her to pick up too many things I dropped or to help with her sister when she's not in the mood, her standard response was, "Yes, but don't call my name for a long, long time!" I appreciated her assertiveness and tried not to take advantage of her kindness and eagerness to help.

On a drive to her dance class one morning, she was not fastened correctly in her child-seat, and when I stopped suddenly, she capitulated forward and banged her head on the metal ramp of my van. When she was in her dance class, apparently, her teacher noticed her bruise. As we were leaving her class, she told me she told her teacher, "My mommy did it!" I was horrified and said, "Oh no, Carissa, don't tell them that I did it. It was an accident." Thinking that was the end of it, she informed me after church the next day she had told the Sunday school teacher, who had also asked about her bruise that "My mommy said not to tell you she did it." I was expecting Social Services to show up any day! Fortunately, that didn't happen. I felt horrible for my carelessness causing the bruise and fortunately learned from it.

My life lesson 13: Appreciate a child's honesty, but be careful of it!

CHAPTER FOURTEEN

Spitfire

Ft. Worth, 1994

We had his-and-her layoffs that year. After two years with Fort Worth Rehabilitation, I had been fortunate in missing the first layoff, but my time finally came. I did not realize hospital administration was changed as often as it was, or I would have stayed at Carter Blood Center. I found a job working half days marketing for Villa Care Inc., a local home health care agency which specialized in services for the disabled community. It gave me more time in the afternoons with the girls and gave me a new appreciation for at-home moms and day care centers. It is hard work entertaining children, especially from a wheelchair. Fortunately, Stephen found another job immediately, so it was a small bump in the road.

Although Cailey had a tough act to follow, she was quite capable with charm and a constant smile. She tolerated almost everything her big sister would dish out. It was obvious when she'd had enough when she would scramble the opposite direction when Carissa approached. Now that Cailey was walking and climbing, she had a fighting chance. From the time Cailey was an infant, she had muscular legs and would fight against receiving the vaccinations from the nurse. This fact helped in many escapes. She was also more curious than her big sister. She would study everything from doorknobs to commode handles, and not give up on figuring things out. She would talk and giggle whenever she got her way—which was most of the time.

After getting laid off twice in two years, I decided in 1994 it was my destiny to stay home. Maybe it was God's way of saying, "Take a load off for a while, and enjoy your children." It was just as well, because keeping up with Carissa's calendar was a full-time job. "We" entered kindergarten and haven't come up for a breath since. She was involved in dance, soccer, and piano. Carissa inherited my impatience and had become anxious about learning to read, driving a car and becoming a mom. She was not sure how she was going to handle it. Her solution was to live with us forever!

Cailey, on the other hand, was not worried about a thing. She has always been my little spitfire two-year-old through and through. She had facial expressions that could either charm the last dollar off you or tell you to get off "her" sidewalk. Cailey was small and mighty and could hold her own with any bully on the playground. I would see nervous mothers wherever we would go because of her daredevil tactics.

My life lesson 14: Acknowledge the differences in your children and love every challenge ahead.

My mom with all the family, now six grandchildren

CHAPTER FIFTEEN

From Seeing Red to Rainbows

Ft. Worth, 1994

I kept on "wheeling" despite life's little ironic twists. I was sued for someone else's neck injuries. Two years earlier while driving my van, I turned right onto a street with railroad tracks traveling approximately fifty feet before I hit the back of a school bus. If I was driving over five miles per hour, I would eat this page. After suffering gentle teasing from friends and coworkers, I had pushed it to the back of my mind. About a month later, a summons arrived at my door! I was being sued by a school aide who was on the bus, and I was ready for some courtroom drama. Can you picture me sitting across from her in my motorized wheelchair with a real neck injury? However, my insurance company settled the case out of court. The woman would not look me in the eye at the official settlement meeting. For a considerable time, whenever I passed a yellow school bus, I would see red!

A highlight of that year was a nanosecond spot on Lifetime Television. They profiled women in the 1990s on a program called *Picture What Women Do*, which included pictures I had submitted of myself with my precious girls—driving the girls to school, diapering Cailey with my teeth, and playing ball with Carissa. If you blinked, you missed it; however, I discovered from a reliable source that they used my television photos on a Fuji commercial. So my fame lived on for a few more Kodak moments! Sorry, Fuji.

An especially insightful moment that same year occurred on a particularly difficult day of fussing at each other. On the way to her piano lesson (which was difficult as both girls never liked going), we saw the most gorgeous rainbow. I mentioned that the rainbow helped me forget about our troubles and Carissa exclaimed that "Rainbows puts color on her heart and made her love everyone." We have discovered that viewing the positives in life helps us find forgiveness and peace.

My life lesson 15: Remember those rainbows
when all you feel is frustration.

CHAPTER SIXTEEN

Kids Say the Darndest Things

Ft. Worth, 1995

If Stephen's birthday in 1995 was any indication of what the year would be like, we should have quit while we were ahead. Carissa had worked hard at decorating his birthday cake. This was unusual since we had always let Kroger bakery make us look good on cakes. She decided to surprise her daddy by hiding the homemade cake in her bedroom. Imagine her carrying the cake in ever so carefully by herself; then add in our big dog, Bo, thinking this baked delight was a treat for him, and you can probably guess what happened. Bo charged for the cake. Carissa took cover, throwing the cake into the air. What we had left was a cake good enough to eat off the floor, Carissa in tears, Stephen figuring out how to save his cake and all of us shocked at how fast it all happened!

I relived my first grade all over again with Carissa—both of us being daydreamers—and having trouble focusing on what the teacher said. After her first day of school, she firmly stated she would do the required task later because she was busy! She didn't like being told what to do, particularly by me. She put me in my place one time by telling me, "My mouth was open all of the time, even when I'm asleep." Translation: I'm always telling her what to do. Carissa was given a fabulous dress-up party on her sixth birthday. Of course, I could not have done it without my mom and Karen. Twenty girls donned high heels, jewelry, fancy dresses, and hats. Karen, our in-house artist, took requests for face painting. These young girls must have recognized the true artist we had on hand because they requested bluebonnets and unicorns!

Cailey still had a look that could put you in your place. Later, she had added vocabulary to it! It wasn't bad language. It was just a tough three-year-old who didn't let anything get in her "big girl" way. She always spoke her mind. One time she was watching a lady at the beauty salon getting her hair dyed. The stylist was applying foil to selected areas of the hair. After several minutes of watching this, Cailey asked, "Why they put trash in her hair like that?"

Between piano and soccer for Carissa and dance lessons for both girls, my only purpose in life seemed to be Chauffeur Extraordinaire. What other mom could roll out a ramp at every stop? After ten years and over 120,000 miles on my big red van, we decided to trade it in and opted for a smaller Ford Windstar. I would still drive right up to the steering wheel; however, this van lowered to the ground with a ramp instead of an electric lift. Hopefully, this would mean fewer mechanical things to go wrong. We used our summer vacation to go pick up the van in Farmington, New Mexico, and to visit Colorado as well.

With a new van to sport around in, I couldn't be seen in an old wheelchair! Stephen had cannibalized every part from my old chair to keep this one running. At my job, my wheelchair would not turn to the right, so during lunch, Stephen just put me up on a cinderblock and replaced a shattered shaft key in one of the driveshafts. Imagine what it might have been like if I hadn't been married to an engineer. With the assistance of insurance and a generous love-filled contribution from my mom, I was in a new wheelchair. This wasn't just any wheelchair. This one had the capability of allowing me to stand up while I'm moving about. Stephen anticipated all the wonderful chores I could perform in the kitchen now. We tested it out at our Sunday school class Christmas party. For the first time in twelve years, I stood socializing face-to-face with dear friends, who could remember how long it had been!

In December of 1995, we had the unique opportunity to be featured in the Sunday edition of our local newspaper, the *Fort Worth Star Telegram*. The writer Carolyn Piorot had known me since my days at Carter Blood Center and said she always found our story newsworthy but never found the time to focus on it. A photographer followed us around on a "typical" day, if there was such a thing in our life, and resulted in a two-page spread. Both Carolyn and Joyce Marshall, the photographer, made our family celebrities for a day. I'm sure my mother was aghast to see Carissa dressed in a nightgown she had worn when I was a child. Talk about your hand-me-downs! With us, "what you see is what you get."

If I could summarize my life during this time in one word, it would be "breakdown" (not mental but mechanical). Although, one may have led to the other! Between my wheelchair and van, both being relatively new, my patience was being tested. But I have learned that trials in life bring new growth opportunities.

Carissa continued to amaze us with her care and sensitivity concerning my disability. At seven and a half years, she could put any home health aide to shame. In a pinch, she could help get me into bed, assist with my clothing, and perform several tasks to complete the process. If there are angels on earth, then I'm, indeed, surrounded. When it came to her chores around the house, though, she often sighed and said she felt like Cinderella. Sometimes, when I asked her to perform a specific task, she would reply, "My hands ran out of gas," or "My legs are too sleepy!" One evening, I attempted for the first time to introduce a discussion of sex and where babies came from with Carissa, and by the time we got to the words *vagina* and *penis*, she was hysterical with the giggles.

Cailey at four constantly amused us with her interpretation of life's mysteries. For instance, when I told her to cover up from the rain, she responded, "Yes, because I don't have as big of an umbrella as God does." She questioned whether we could see angels; after all, we see them on the television show *Touched by an Angel*. At Carissa's spring choir musical, Cailey had us in stitches when she commented as a young girl tore off the pages of an easel, "Boy, she does good work!" It is a small wonder kids can teach adults to appreciate the small stuff like appreciating the minor parts played in a musical. Cailey started telling me, "She could do things with her power (imagination)." I discovered Carissa was the one who got her started on it one day (when she was too busy to pay attention to her little sister). She made this up and told Cailey she would watch her with "her power."

Our summer vacation consisted of driving to Stephen's grandparents in Kansas and then to his parents in Chicago, as well as a fun stop at Branson, Missouri, for a few spectacular shows and rides at Silver Dollar City. Homeward bound, however, turned out to be a hair-raising event beginning with me accidentally running over my mother-in-law Carol's new four-month-old kitten with my wheelchair. Then in St. Louis, our brakes went out on the exit ramp to our hotel. As luck would have it, the part needed to repair the brakes was out of stock. Our theme for the year with this van had been "If we had no bad luck, we'd have no luck at all!" Somehow, we managed to rent the last available wheelchair accessible van to get back home. Since this was quite a blow to the pocketbook, I hadn't decided if it was luck. I think the kitten fared better than we did with no broken bones. Next summer, the cat steered clear of my wheelchair.

Another highlight of the year was the opportunity to show off our family in a national magazine in May, even if, in my opinion, it bordered on being a tabloid! *Women's World* took great pictures but overdramatized my plight a bit. I gave them anecdotes and funny situations we found ourselves in. They wrote a story using words like *agony* and *despair*. Speaking of situations I found myself in, how about this one? One of the fun things I could do in this new wheelchair was stand up. However, one day, I discovered the switch that operates the standing frame could go out while I'm standing! Yes, I was stuck and couldn't sit down. Not a good predicament for a quadriplegic with low blood pressure. Cailey came to my rescue with a portable phone, which enabled me to call a neighbor. My neighbor was one of those angels I was talking about, and Dennis Ford (who was home and had recently recovered from a heart attack) was there in a "heartbeat" for assistance. Stephen was on the way home and ultimately pulled me from the chair until they could get it down. Later that same month, my gear box went out, and the chair wouldn't turn to the left. I could only go in circles! Also, I rode around in my manual chair with two flat tires! I'm sure this all tested my sense of humor. We wouldn't trade our dilemmas for anyone else's in the world. We were blessed and secure in God's love.

My life lesson 16: Babies are a piece of God we get to hold.
(Carissa's godparents gave us this message on a plaque, and
it continues to be a special decoration in my house.)

Cailey and Carissa with Cherie, *Ft. Worth Star Telegram* article, 1995

CHAPTER SEVENTEEN

I've Survived Darned Near Everything

Fossil Rim Wildlife Center, 1997

One reason I decided to write my book was to share the outrageous and, in hindsight, the comical situations that resulted, most of which involve my van or wheelchair malfunctioning. My case in point is what I call Nightmare at Fossil Rim! When my sister Karen and her daughter Dani came for the weekend in the spring of 1997, the highlight of the trip was to visit our granddaddy Dixon in Granbury and sightsee at Fossil Rim, an animal kingdom located in the cliffs near Granbury. We could not have asked for better weather; unfortunately, that later created havoc with my car.

The trouble began at the first sign, "Steep Grade Ahead." As we made our way up the "steep grade," my van sputtered, and the engine died. I started groaning, and the girls began whimpering. At the first sign of any trouble, our "fearless" Cailey, who had been with me on several breakdowns, panics first and asks questions later. We managed to get a little farther up the hill, and then the engine died again, and we lost the power brakes and steering! We rolled backward with all three girls screaming, "We're going to die!" with their eyes covered and me yelling for Karen to grab my emergency brake, which was virtually impossible for her to reach. We landed in a ditch, which was a better alternative than careening over the edge of the cliff or pounding into the car behind us, which had wisely backed up! Karen felt sure we were heading for death off the cliff, so she was a nervous wreck. I, on the other hand, had just added another adventure to my top ten list of "You know it's a bad day when..." We called the Park

Services, and they came to our rescue by pulling us from the ditch. They took good care of us. They refunded our entire admission and any gift items we had purchased. However, this was not the end of our woes. On the way back to my aunt Patricia's with her following us, the van sputtered and died again. Fortunately, Patricia was there to help and called the Ford Company. They felt the problem was some winterized gasoline creating a vacuum in the gas line which, in turn, caused the engine to stall. Once the gas cap was removed, the vacuum was relieved, and the van drove fine from that point.

On the way home, all thoughts turned to thankfulness. Carissa commented, "If you don't love God, bad things will happen." After several insightful moments, Dani responded, "I love God!" Dani went on to say, "God lives in heaven," to which Carissa added, "I thought I saw heaven once, but Daddy told me it was just a jet stream from an airplane." Cailey had her moments with God as well. With any crisis, she automatically dropped to her knees and prayed that God would make her mom walk; perhaps believing if I could walk, I would be able avoid these ridiculous situations!

We didn't manage to escape another van breakdown. On a trip, coming back from Houston for my high school twenty-year reunion, the van did the same sputter-and-die routine, except this time it didn't start again. It turned into another adventure with all of us riding in the van on a flatbed wrecker to the Hempstead vehicle impound yard, where we waited for Stephen to take a taxi to the car rental agency. At least we discovered the source of our troubles. The first diagnosis was winterized gas causing a vapor lock. This time, it was the fuel pump. Our attitude had become "It's nothing $500 (or more) won't fix!"

I cannot remember a year when mechanical problems—wheelchair or van—have not been a part of our lives, and 1997 was no different. The good news was this time at the very least we were not left stranded on the highway, and since the repair was due to a recall, we didn't have to dedicate our Christmas budget to the Ford Motor Company. The bad news is I am useless without either one of my "wheels" (van or wheelchair), and I had been without both and resorting to a manual wheelchair which really limits my independence.

One form of transportation Stephen and I enjoyed was a Caribbean cruise! We flew to Puerto Rico and from there sailed to St. Thomas and St. Martin. We were scheduled to visit St. Croix as well but could not dock that morning. This was all to celebrate Stephen and I both turning forty and our ten years of marriage. It was a week of relaxation, great food, entertaining waiters, meeting interesting people from other parts of the country, and no parental responsibilities for the time being. It was a good thing we celebrated fifteen years on the cruise because there were some tense moments when our alma maters, Kansas State (his) and the Texas Aggies (mine), played for the Big 12 Championship. Stephen didn't speak for at least an hour after his Wildcat loss, and no one dared utter a "Gig'em" (an Aggie expression) for at least a week. Cailey, always the astute one, put him in his place in one of his gloating moments during the game commenting that "It wasn't like *he* was going to get a trophy or anything!"

My life lesson 17: You can learn many insightful things
when kids do not realize you are listening.

CHAPTER EIGHTEEN

Those Who Can't Make Others Do It

Ft. Worth, 1998

One of the things, if any at all, I can claim for success in my children was keeping them busy with activities. Since I couldn't do it, I would live vicariously through them. Carissa's included dance, soccer, and the dreaded piano lessons. The year before she had stated she would rather be blind! At least this year as they say, "Misery loves company." Cailey shared the torture of piano lessons with her. We now had the pleasure of hearing whining about piano practice in stereo. Cailey was involved in soccer and gymnastics, as well as the piano. We had become accustomed to hearing, "Who's that little blonde girl?" on the soccer field. She was also popular on the playground where she spins the other kids fast and furiously in the tire. She said with utmost seriousness, "Kids depend upon her." I even witnessed a second-grade boy seeking her out one day to ask if she would push him. Other moms applaud scholastic prowess in their children. I applaud playground prowess!

Cailey had become a paranoid passenger when it came to my van. This year, she didn't escape one of my "situations." This time, it was at the car wash where we got one-third of the way in when my front tire blew out! As we were sitting there with the water continuing to spray, Cailey said with a pitiful voice and expression, "Are we ever going to get out of here?" Following this incident, she would not go to the car wash with me anymore!

With great sadness, we had to put both Dudley, our cat, and Bo, our dog, to permanent rest within the same year. Dudley had been with me since my senior year in college—seventeen years ago! He was also the survivalist cat in our car accident, so you can imagine how he ranked in the household. We would also miss how Bo would gaze lovingly at Stephen (as though he was the one who invented bones). On a happier note, we were not long without animals. Carissa's godparents gave us two kittens, Rascal and Sweetie. At this point, we should have invested in our vet's practice, as those free kittens had a way of adding up in cost. As with all our beloved pets throughout my experience, they were worth it.

During our visit to the Cotner's in Naperville, Illinois, I managed to avoid running over her cat. Rascal wasn't as lucky. It wasn't like I seek out kittens to run over, as my history of doing so would indicate. I just don't think to look underneath before I take off. I backed over Rascal as I was leaving my desk and relived the cat's screech in my sleep for months. Fortunately, it only took once for the cats to learn, or I might have PETA hunting me down for cruelty. When Cailey was a baby, she had gotten behind my wheelchair and was so quiet I had not realized she was there before I backed up. Cailey's little cry didn't compare to the cat screech, but I felt ten times worse. Stephen grabbed Cailey and started calming her, and Carissa immediately sensed my anxiety and remorse and came to comfort me. Fortunately, both kittens and babies are resilient!

My life lesson 18: Even though you may not see the humor at the moment, this verse has been a cornerstone from Proverbs 31:25, "She is clothed with strength and dignity; she can laugh at the days to come."

THINGS YOU ALWAYS WANTED TO ASK A QUAD BUT WERE AFRAID TO:

Do you ever get depressed?

I would be lying if I said no. I have my moments of feeling depressed or feeling sorry for myself. I try to keep these at a minimum and to myself. My daughters are the ones who have witnessed the occasional tantrum or crying mainly from frustration rather than depression. I particularly get upset when I spill the dog treats. Angel gets a bonus on those days! I would say that frustration is my strongest emotion to describe bad moments.

How did you have children?

As I mentioned in chapter 10, "we did the old-fashioned way." By this I mean I can still perform sex. However, I do not experience the sensation anymore. The doctor told me after my car accident that we could still have children but to wait for at least five years. That is exactly what we did. I stopped taking my birth control, and within six to eight months of sexual intercourse, we discovered I was pregnant! I took a home pregnancy test the weekend of my sister, Karen's wedding, and announced the exciting news after the festivities concluded. Both my children were born naturally, not by Cesarean as many believe.

Why do you always have crumbs on your lap?

My daughter Cailey often wondered why I always had crumbs on my lap until she performed a project for school her senior year.

She pushed herself around in a manual wheelchair all day to feel what it was like for a person with a disability. She discovered that there was no other place else for the crumbs to fall!

Does it hurt? Or what does it feel like?

Believe it or not, I have had nurses, caregivers, and even doctors ask me this. I have no sensation from the chest down and sporadic feeling in my arms. Most of all, I just feel a tingling sensation throughout my body. My only explanation for them asking me this is they forget about my disability when asking the question.

How do you pee and poop?

This was the most difficult change in my body to accept. The capability to urinate and poop would forever be on schedule! For five years after the accident, I would intermittently catheterize every four hours. This was a royal pain as it would require me coming home from work in the middle of the day. I was also invariably wet in between. Once I got pregnant, I switched to an indwelling catheter, which made my life so much more flexible. It may sound crazy; but I only poop on Monday, Wednesday, and Friday with the help of a suppository to help stimulate the process. Another advantage is I don't have to "run" for a bathroom anymore. Everything is scheduled which makes travel more complicated.

What do you miss the most since your accident?

I was athletic before the accident, so the easy answer would be running and dancing. I would run five miles per day and often participated in aerobic dance at the gym before or after work. Presently, I stay fit with an exercise called REFIT®. I meet twice a week with a group of women and exercise for an hour to Christian songs like "Unfinished" and motivational songs like "Never Give Up." Although I can only exercise the upper body, it elevates my heart rate and makes me feel great following the workout and devotional. Although I can dance from the wheelchair, I miss group or line dances like "The Hustle" and country western dancing. It may seem trivial, but I miss simply crossing my legs. I also participate in Sheng Zhen meditation. I was privileged to participate in a workshop with the world-renowned Master Li Junfeng. (If you Google his name, you will see why it was an honor to be in his presence.) He commented that "I did not move well compared to the rest of the group, but I always had smile on my face!"

If you could have one thing back, what would it be?

What I often tell people is appreciate your finger movement. I miss the ability to just pick up a pen and write without having to put on a hand splint. The wheelchair and not being able to walk I can handle, but if I had to make a choice between my upper or lower body to work again, I would choose my hand and finger movement. I required my hand splint during the initial years of my injury to eat meals and to write with a pen. With time and experience, I have learned to use utensils and a pen without the hand splints. But I still require the splints for putting on makeup.

Has the disability changed you as a person?

That is a difficult one to answer because I had just become a young adult when my accident happened. I would say my confidence was most affected, especially when applying for jobs. I constantly worried what the person was thinking about my capabilities. I knew given the chance I could prove myself but was not given the opportunity on multiple interviews. One important thing has not changed, and that is my perseverance. It got me through college when challenged, and it helped me through the daily struggles with my disability. I have become more faithful and confident that God has blessed me as a result of my gratitude for these challenges.

CHAPTER NINETEEN

Never Say Never

Ft. Worth, 1999

Never in my wildest dreams could I imagine how 1999 would end. My life became like the soap operas I watched daily. Before I get to the details of my personal nightmare, I'd be remiss to skip over our fun trip to Disney World in the summer of that year. Stephen's parents had generously donated their timeshare in Orlando for us to use while we spent five glorious days visiting the various parks and attractions. Carissa was ten years old and Cailey six and a half years old. Whereas Carissa was big enough to get on all of the rides, Cailey's small size prevented her from riding several of the roller coasters—which made her angry at being left behind with me to hold her. However, there were two roller coasters we all got to ride on. The scariest ride was Space Mountain, where it was totally dark inside. Even though I knew Cailey was safe with Stephen (holding her in the car behind me), I could not hear or see her, and it was driving this overprotective mom berserk. It was a great treat for me since I had not been on a roller coaster since high school. It brought back wonderful memories at AstroWorld in Houston, when I had the freedom to run from ride to ride. Now Stephen transferred me on and off the rides throughout the trip. Another favorite ride we all could enjoy was the Twilight Zone Tower of Terror, the one where you feel as though you're dropping two hundred feet on an elevator. We did that several times during the day! We also enjoyed the amenities of the condominium and lying out by the pool.

Now for the hard part, because later I discovered Stephen had started an affair before we had left for our "family" vacation. It started off as most affairs do, with him getting home late and coming up with creative excuses. In August, he had to go to Austin on "business." Only later, I would discover a flower arrangement which was sent to the hotel on the weekend he was in Austin was charged on our credit card. Several nights, he claimed to be working late. My favorite reasons for his lateness, which were just begging to be exposed, were when he said he was at Osmond's Sporting Goods until 10:00 p.m. (which closed at 9:00 p.m. back then) and when he said he stopped at Barnes and Noble to watch a sports event on their big-screen television (which was nowhere to be found). Then on a Saturday, he laid me down to nap and left the house at 4:00 p.m. without saying anything to anyone. He returned at 8:00 p.m. Carissa had to get me back up from my nap, since we had no idea when he was going to come home! Later, he said he was at a Sports Bar watching the K-State game with buddies from work.

When I found the credit card charge for flowers, I finally confronted Stephen and forced him to admit to his duplicity. He tried to deny it at first, stating the charge was there by mistake. I went to the phone to confirm the charge, and he decided he could fool me no longer. He would not reveal who the affair was with, but I knew it was someone in our church choir! The ironic part of this story is that I was the one who encouraged him to join the choir because I knew he had a love of singing dating back to his fraternity days in college. He would sing some of his more acceptable fraternity songs as lullabies to the girls at night.

I admit there were many Sundays I spent glaring at several women in the choir, wondering which one was the home-wrecker! I discovered it was in fact a choir member, Melissa, with whom he had spent many choir practices, extending their nights into an affair. I called my sister, Karen, in tears later with my discovery. Sadly, she and my sister-in-law, Jo Ella, already had their suspicions about his fidelity. Being an Air Force wife, Jo Ella said she could spot a man beginning an affair because he would lose weight and focus more on his appearance. True to form, Stephen had lost a lot of weight and was looking better than he had in the past few years. I lost weight for other reasons. I lost my appetite and cried for fear of what lay ahead and believing the doubts that Stephen began putting in my head about raising the girls on my own.

When we met with a counselor, Steve focused on how this other relationship was good for his ego and would help him move into management. He didn't want to be in a dependent relationship (my physical dependence on him); instead he wanted an equal partnership. The counselor stressed he was focusing on a negative relationship with me and not giving it a chance. He said he would never feel sexual fulfillment with me, and he felt he would continue to lust after other women! She stated Stephen would have to decide about staying and making positive changes. Otherwise, he would take these negative feelings with him to the next relationship. She also pointed out the baggage it would bring into future relationships since it would be entered under lies and deceit. He talked about his unhappiness and that I didn't meet his needs. Then he went on to tell me later how this other woman energized him and had made him more of an extrovert! I realize that it takes two in a marriage and blame can land on each side. On my side, I'm sure I was putting more of my attention on Carissa and Cailey but honestly did not see what was coming as a result.

When he found out I was planning on moving to Houston to be close to my family, he approached me with a budget. It was divided into two columns detailing expenses each of us would pay. He said if I stayed in town, he would help pay; otherwise, I'd be on my own. He would fight for custody. He stated he was going to look for apartments. I left the room and broke down. The girls came in and hugged me. Stephen came in and put his arms around us, but Carissa told him to take his hands off because he didn't want to be a part of this family. He called everyone in back together and asked if he dropped this other woman would we all forgive and take him back. We all said we would and discussed some of the changes we needed to make. He asked what we all felt about adopting a baby boy. I responded we had a relationship to repair and to get this family healthy before that issue could be addressed.

We spent Thanksgiving in Naperville, Illinois. Stephen stated that this would be a time for us to work things out and he would talk to his family. He blew up on the day before Thanksgiving when we were going to Chicago to shop simply because the girls were wearing jeans and he didn't think they looked nice enough. He said this was why he was getting out of this family—that he didn't want to live like this anymore and he wanted better for himself.

We took the girls upstairs and told them he would be seeking a divorce. Carissa responded in tears. Throughout the week, Stephen called Melissa on his cell phone, and when the girls asked who he was talking to, he would always say he was checking his voice mail. Carissa tried to hide his cell phone several times. Late that night or early morning, Stephen heard Cailey crying and found she had wet the bed again. He felt guilty about her crying and brought her to my bed, and all four of us slept in the same bed that night. Stephen expressed how he didn't want to be responsible for her unhappiness.

The day after Thanksgiving, Stephen changed gears again and said he wanted the divorce. He said no court would give a woman in a wheelchair custody of the kids. This stirred many angry emotions, so I let him know I had hired a lawyer. He got real belligerent and said he wasn't going to shower me, but he came back and continued talking until he calmed down and then took care of me. I lost weight from the stress of worrying and wondering what the future would bring. I was frightened about his threats of taking me to court for the girls. He was successful in creating doubts in my mind about my taking care of them on my own. I knew I had great family and friends as a support network which gave me the strength to carry on. I understand many women have experienced divorce. My situation was more complicated because of my disability and my dependence upon Stephen the previous sixteen years.

You can see the emotional abuse I suffered. It was like a roller coaster with him changing his mind at every turn. The last straw was on December 17. At lunch, Stephen told the girls he wanted to stay committed to this family and he was going to break up with Melissa after the choir party that night. He told me he wanted to get his things out of her apartment. That night, he went to both his company

Christmas party and the choir Christmas party alone and returned home about 10:30 p.m. to 11:00 p.m. He had to go back out for groceries. During that time, Melissa started calling on the fax line (a signal for him to call her). When he didn't call, she called our main line and hung up. Then she called the fax line a few more times and called back on our line again and asked for Stephen. I said he wasn't home and immediately hung up. She arrived at our house when Stephen drove up from the grocery store and demanded her key back. He told her he would be over later. He told me he could either stay with this family or go live with Melissa and, without further comment, started packing a few things. I started crying and telling him I was tired of the emotional roller coaster he had put this family through with his mind changes day to day. He stopped packing. Melissa later came to the door about 12:30 a.m. and knocked. I told Stephen he should ignore her. She then started pounding on the door and ringing the bell continuously. She left and started calling the fax line again, returned at 1:15 a.m., and once again started ringing the doorbell nonstop. At this point, I called the police and reported her actions. She proceeded to Carissa's front window, where she pounded, waking Carissa up and scaring her half to death. Carissa screamed and ran to our room. Melissa came around to the side of the house where she started yelling through our window that Stephen had ruined *her* life and he had tried to screw seven altos in the choir before her! As she pounded, she broke the window, and her hand came through. At this point, I didn't know what she was going to do, so I said that the police were on the way, and she left. We followed up with a report to the police. A Detective Phillips called to follow up on our complaint. He called Melissa with a warning that we would file charges if she contacted us again. She said it wouldn't be a problem.

We went our separate ways at Christmas. The girls and I felt positive after the scene Melissa pulled before the holidays, he would have nothing more to do with her. However, as soon as we returned from Houston, the lies continued. Just to confirm my suspicions, I followed him and saw him drive into Melissa's apartment complex. When asked why he returned late, he lied once again and said he went for a beer after his meeting. He threatened later to contest the divorce since I was quadriplegic and couldn't take care of myself, much less the girls. He said I was trying to get too much, wouldn't agree to the settlement, and would spend all the money before I got it. He later apologized and said he would not contest it. He moved in with Melissa that night. That pretty much sealed our fate, as I felt the marriage could not be saved. How could I ever trust a man who continued to be deceitful and more concerned with his relationship with another woman than his own children? Furthermore, he had not expressed any guilt or remorse.

I had attempted marriage counseling. There did not seem to be any guilt or remorse on his part. I had also met with a female pastor at my church. She had advised it was not healthy for my daughters to see their father treating women like he did. I, therefore, took the steps necessary to continue with the divorce and, with my family's help, started the process of moving to Houston. When Stephen realized I was serious about leaving, he asked if I would consider giving him a second chance. He said I could check on him at lunch to see if he was coming home on time after work, and other ridiculous scenarios in which I had to "police" the marriage. I decided I did not want to live that way—constantly questioning whether he was being trustworthy from one day to the next. After the hurtful things he had already said, I found it impossible to stay. The hardest part would be leaving my dear friends of over sixteen years. We had joined a Couples Bible Class called "Koinonia" when we became members of First United Methodist Church. These friends were a lifeline throughout many of my challenging days. But it would not be right to leave this chapter without expressing what their generosity meant to me during that time. They all got together as a class and paid for my moving expenses! It was an unpredictable, scary time for me as I don't like change in my schedule and I certainly wasn't financially stable. The best way I can thank them is through recognizing their efforts in my book. Another critical link back then was with the parents at All Saints Episcopal School, where the girls went to school. Many of our friends had gotten together to have a "moving shower." They were very generous in giving us household items we would need in our new home. Carissa and Cailey were given bright-yellow shirts all their friends from school had signed. It was more difficult than I can adequately describe in words, leaving all the wonderful relationships we had been blessed with in the sixteen years we had lived in Ft. Worth.

How ironic I had sent this fax to a radio station just months before I discovered the affair:

May 17, 1999

Dear Banana Joe, Anna & the Jamming Magic 102 Team!

If there was anyone who deserves a break, I believe it's my husband, Stephen, who I've been married to sixteen years this coming July 9th. We had the idyllic wedding with the typical vows where you promise to love in sickness and in health. Six months later those vows were tested when we had a car accident resulting in my being paralyzed with a neck injury, leaving me quadriplegic. I spent five months of our newlywed year in a rehabilitation hospital in Dallas. Stephen drove 100 miles round trip each day, after working 8 hours, to provide the encouragement, support and love I needed to survive this challenging time. The fact he stuck around after this tragic accident is amazing for the statistics show otherwise, especially when we only knew each other eight months before we married. Well, not only has he stuck around, but we've gone on to have two beautiful daughters, Carissa (10) and Cailey (6 and 1/2), who also "jam" with you and love your "Friday throw-downs." Stephen is a busy man, since he has always been my caregiver. When the girls were younger, he shouldered that responsibility as well. As you can imagine, he doesn't get much time to relax. I'd love to give

him this cruise as a way of thanks for his love and
commitment. Even after the constant challenge
of my disability and the care of two active children, romance is still a vital part of our relationship. Jamming with you guys on this cruise will
be an adventure we'd love to experience!

P.S. If you read my fax while I'm driving, be
patient for my call. I drive with hand controls
and must stop the car to call you!

Following the divorce, Melissa broke up with Stephen. I could
relate to the words in the song "Jolene" by Dolly Parton, "I'm begging of you please don't take my man, Jolene (Melissa). Don't take
him just because you can." As difficult as it might have been, my
family didn't disrespect Stephen in front of my girls following the
divorce. One of the hardest things about moving to Houston was
disrupting their current circumstances and leaving their friends when
we moved to Houston. Once we arrived, I did find a counselor to
help them through the emotional aspects of divorce. Another detail
I had feared was the financial one of being on my own with no job
prospects on the horizon. Fortunately, through mediation, Stephen
agreed to pay five years of alimony to help me until I was employed.

Even though my fear of Stephen leaving came true, I pray this
chapter has not overshadowed all the blessings Stephen provided since
the car accident. Forgiveness has been essential with both the accident
and the divorce. Despite my frustration and anger with Stephen, forgiveness has given me more peace of mind through numerous Bible
studies and talking with women in similar situations.

*My life lesson 19: I had now learned the true meaning of
"Never say never!" I never thought it could happen after all
we had been through together, but it had, and now it was
time to move on. My theme song has always been as Helen
Reddy sings, "I am woman. Hear me roar!" The first time I
heard her sing it, I knew it would be my mantra for life!*

POSITIVE THINGS ABOUT BEING A QUADRIPLEGIC:

- Soft hands from not doing much work with them
- No waiting in line at Disney World
- Parking spaces available up front
- My thunder thighs—keeping muscular now; hindrance when I was self-conscious about my legs
- Not growing tired from too much walking. Can't remember how many times I've heard in the store, "I need one of those."
- Weight—constantly struggled with weight most of my life. But because of muscle spasms, I have maintained same weight for almost thirty years with little or no exercise; spasms burn calories.
- Can drive a car, and it's like a kid magnet.
- I believe God has a sense of humor. I always wanted to be taller than my five-foot-two height and didn't like the size of my butt. In the wheelchair, I appear to be taller, and no one sees my big butt!

CHAPTER TWENTY

Starting Over

Cobblestone Drive, Houston, Texas, 2000

We arrived in Houston to move in during the Memorial Day weekend of 2000. It could not have been accomplished without several weekends of prior help from friends, my two sisters Karen and Kathryn, and my mom. On the other end, my brother Bob, my sister-in-law Jo Ella, and my brother-in-law Tom were waiting for Karen and Kathy to join them when the movers arrived on Tuesday to unload. I believe the girls went ahead with Karen, and my mom rode with me in my van. To say the timing was planned practically to the minute is understated. The moving company made the mistake of telling my family they could not make it on Tuesday. I don't know what was said to convince them, but the president of the moving company drove the van to Houston himself! All the work done beforehand—the decorating, remodeling the bathroom to fit my needs, and lawn care—was a true labor of love by all involved.

Both girls adjusted well to their new schools. Carissa hardly missed a beat as she plunged in and met the challenge with her organizational and life skills learned at All Saints Episcopal School. As she approached adolescence, I felt the generational gap widen when we listened to her CDs. I was constantly asking, "What are they saying?" I'm not sure if having to ask or discovering what they were saying bothered me more. Cailey got a reputation during her first week of school that she liked to race and don't let her size fool you! One of the boy's moms told me he came home and said there was a new girl at school challenging the boys on the track and winning! She was never at a loss for friends because she would enjoy walking around the backyard in conversation with her imaginary ones. Carissa decided she would give guitar lessons a try, and Cailey would attempt violin lessons. This proved to be a challenge for us all since it involved parent involvement from their tone-deaf mom. Throughout the new transitions we faced, this motto got us through it, "Life is 10 percent what you make it and 90 percent how you take it."

We had one crazy night when I woke up from a nightmare in which I dreamed I was under attack in a basement and screamed as loud as my lungs would allow. You must remember that once I am in bed, I cannot simply stand and move. Carissa came running from her room. Cailey, who was asleep beside me, covered her head, most likely scared of what was occurring. I was still in a dream state and thought she was my attacker and told Carissa to call the police. She was too frightened, so I was dialing 911 when an operator answered. Fortunately, I woke up and realized it was just a nightmare and assured the operator we were okay. After things settled down, we laughed to the point of tears and have had many laughs over the memory since then.

As we were settled in our new environment, I knew I could lean on my family for challenges and emergencies—which occur more frequently than I care to admit. I relied upon my brother Bob as he was always "on call" for van shuttle to the repair shop. My sister Karen and sister-in-law Jo Ella and my mom were backup carpools and substitute moms. Karen's husband, Tom, was and would always be my number one repair guru. This was the primary reason we had to leave Ft. Worth and chose Houston to live in.

One major change that occurred in 2001 was going back to work after being a stay-at-home mom for almost nine years. I was nervous about how this would affect Carissa and Cailey with me not being home when they returned from school. With the alimony stopping in a few years, I had to consider the help the income would provide our family. Karen noticed a new SAM'S Club which would be built that year and suggested I apply. I did apply, and the next thing I knew I was employed in the marketing department calling on businesses in the area for membership. It took a couple of months for them to get used to me and the fact I can be teased about my disability. But soon enough, it was said in fun, "I was always sitting around on the job," and many were threatened with the "Quad Slap" which a coworker described as holding my hand up and a person running into it!

My life lesson 20: Change can be scary or exciting, but either way, it's inevitable. It's your choice how to deal with it.

CHAPTER TWENTY-ONE

Believe It or Not—Dumb Luck

Houston, 2002

The year would not be complete without a crazy transportation incident. As had been the case so often, Cailey was with me on this one as well. She got a "free ride" as many would comment because she was small enough to ride on the back of my wheelchair. We were crossing the parking lot into a store, traveling at my usual top speed, when suddenly my wheelchair spun out of control in a circle and stopped as the left front wheel came completely off! I had experienced several flats but had never lost a wheel while driving. I don't know who was more stunned, but Cailey was the first to say with a quiver, "What are we going to do now, Mom?" Well, a kind couple who had been taking their own disabled son out of their car and witnessed me spinning out of control took charge and helped in our distress. They tilted me over and pounded that tire back on and, when the chair would not respond to turning left, guided me back to the van. When I got home, my repair guru, Tom, replaced a broken bolt (which took three stores to find) for fifty cents. If I had gone to a wheelchair shop for the repair, I'm sure it would have cost fifty to a hundred dollars.

In 2002, Carissa was thirteen, going on thirty! I don't exaggerate. She had always been more mature for her age because of my situation, and she truly was a big help to me in so many ways. Unfortunately, we didn't get to miss out on the emotional extremes of a teenager who lamented about having to deal with an out-of-touch mom and a pesky little sister! Fortunately, she had plenty to keep her busy and her mind off boys or drugs! She was in the eighth grade, her final year at Memorial Middle School, where she still thrived in Musical Theater. She also enjoyed classes in dance and sewing. Carissa was still with the Albion Hurricane soccer team as forward/midfielder. We would endure the stress of practices and lost Saturdays since she enjoyed the game. We had the eighth-grade dance to anticipate for that spring, which I understand equates to a high school prom! Hopefully, I would receive a nice tax refund to pay for the dress! Otherwise, babysitting and dog sitting would be in Carissa's future.

Cailey was ten, and in the fourth grade at Frostwood Elementary. Believe it or not, she was still in the violin program. The only problem that year seemed to be her private lesson took the place of her recess once a week, and she forgot to go to her violin lesson. The teacher had to track her down on the playground! She gave up gymnastics for the time being but was still playing soccer as midfielder with the Westside Stars. If I had more money and time, she'd have been in more sports! She had a creative spark that had always been interesting to observe. Her room was always a mess with her in-progress projects, but her Mimi gave her room a facelift that year by buying a new bed with drawers for storage and a wardrobe to get some of the "junk" off her floor. We were not expecting miracles, but we saw improvement.

As for me, I was still with Sam's. I managed to get a few hours in between the girls' activities and my doctor appointments! That year had been the most challenging year with my health. You'd think I was in gymnastics with as many times I've "rolled" or fallen out of my wheelchair! I've had so many muscle spasms I resorted to tying my ankles to the wheelchair footrest to keep them in place. I had stopped worrying about the stares I got months earlier. Let them wonder.

In 2003, I was approved once again to have a van modified by the Texas Rehabilitation Commission (TRC). The process started in May with my purchasing a new 2003 Dodge Caravan. The tricky part was purchasing the van before the paperwork went to Austin for approval. Fortunately, we had the help of my cousin, Representative Dennis Bonnen, in Austin to nudge the approval process along. My mother helped with paying off my old van so I wouldn't have two car payments. We waited patiently while the new van was modified, until it was finally shipped and received in September. The reason I described the process is I do not know how people survive the ordeal without assistance as I was blessed with. The updated version in this van was the sliding door on the driver's side, for the girls to use, instead of having to enter or exit through my door with the ramp. As the girls had grown older, my van had become less of a "cool space-ship" and more of a nuisance. It was always a pain when dropping off one of them from the backseat.

I had finally added a seat belt to my wheelchair since I had somersaulted out of my wheelchair four times already. The first was my experience with Cailey when I spun out of control in the parking lot. I then hit a tree stump in front of Karen's house. The wheel-chair stopped, and I flipped out and onto the yard—thankfully not the driveway. Karen and the girls had gone next door to look at the neighbor's new dog, and so I was alone for a few minutes, yelling piti-fully for help since my lung capacity has never been great since my accident. I had a mild incident of hitting the door hinge and falling forward more gently to the carpeted floor in my house, and Carissa and Cailey picking me up off the floor and putting me back in the chair. The last time was the most humiliating episode. I was zipping through SAM'S Club at my usual ninety-to-nothing speed when one minute I was moving and the very next minute I was catapulted to the cement floor when the front left wheelchair tire fell off! A kind customer sat and held my head in their lap while another wheelchair could be found to transfer me into. It was amazing I didn't reinjure my spinal cord. My body ached for days. I believe the company who sold me the wheelchair was worried I would sue, so they gladly refur-bished my wheelchair, making it look like new again.

My life lesson 21: When life throws you somersaults, respond with a "Weeee."

CHAPTER TWENTY-TWO

These Boots Aren't Made for Walking

Houston, 2004

One of the most memorable aspects of '04 for me personally was the challenge to my health. My muscle spasms increased as the result of a wound. The wound took nearly three months to heal, and I was hospitalized for the first time since my injury—nothing serious. The doctor just wanted me monitored during IV treatment for an infection. To finish off the year, I got a pressure sore on the back of the heal and had to wear a "stylish" boot for pressure relief. Many observers believed I was in the wheelchair because of a foot injury. I'm flattered to be mistaken for someone who could walk.

Carissa was so busy at this point in high school with soccer and Markettes (drill team) it was amazing she had any time left for homework! She was also doing her driver education online (Driver in a Box!) with her dad responsible for the driving instruction while she was with him in California. Although I was not in any hurry for her to experience Houston traffic, I knew she would want her driver's license by the time she turned sixteen.

Along with Albion soccer, Cailey had added gymnastics to the mix. She loved gymnastics because it did not require "practice." She got a "do-over" on the desk in her bedroom as a Christmas gift from Mimi, anticipating improved homework habits in the New Year! She got asked to do a commercial last summer while out in California, but I was "mean" and wouldn't let her do it, or as Cailey would tell you, "I ruined her career!"

As Carissa was in her teens and Cailey fast approaching, I thought back to the wise advice my parents tried to give me. My dad once told me how time passes relative to your age and, as you got older, how much faster it passed. I'm sure it was a lesson on appreciating life and not wishing my life away. I probably didn't appreciate it then, but as I approached fifty, "Boy, I did then!" I was at the age, when my parents were in their fifties, where I was worried about them dying! Tragically, my father did die of a heart attack at age fifty-four. At seventy-four, my mom looked vital and too young to have three adult children in their fifties and one at age sixty!

To cheer us up from the loss of our cat Rascal, Karen surprised me when she picked us up in a forty-two-foot Escalade Limousine and took us and the rest of the family to the Water Wall at the Galleria. A quote I liked this year said it best about keeping a positive attitude: "To the world, you may be one person, but to one person, you may be the world!"

My life lesson 22: Wouldn't it be nice if life came with "practice" sessions and we could have "do-overs"?

CHAPTER TWENTY-THREE

Fire Brigade

Three Spur Ranch, Anderson, Texas, 2005

On July 2, 2005, my family hosted a "Bratz & Beer" party at my mom's Three Spur Ranch in Anderson, Texas. We celebrated the patriotic holiday with live music from The Moe Hansum Band. It was a fun day of camaraderie, horseshoes, delicious food, and fireworks! It was a good thing Mimi had the foresight to have a "fire truck" close by (her pickup truck with a fifty-gallon barrel of water in the back end). The fireworks began shooting across the pasture instead of toward the sky. Consequently, it created several fires in the process. The fire brigade consisted of Mimi, Karen, Tom, and Clay with their rakes and water! Fortunately, the band played a little louder, and not too many guests were even aware of the mishap. Even though I write humorously about it in hindsight, it came close to putting Karen's eye out. Tom, our safety expert, refined the protocol for future events!

Just about the time I thought I was going to make it a year without something crazy happening, I had the misfortune of deploying my ramp down on the street as an elderly woman drove by, and she ran over the ramp! The ramp was damaged on the lower half but fortunately remained functional. To top off this ridiculous episode, she blamed me because I didn't have a flag on it, and she claimed it looked just like the ground! She did come through, however, and reported to her insurance. It was repaired rather quickly and inexpensively.

We did add another addition to the household that year. In November, Cailey picked out a four-month-old kitten, Pepper, from

CAP (Citizens for Animal Protection) as an early Christmas gift. She had always wanted to get a kitten after we lost Rascal several years earlier. I had been putting it off long as possible but finally gave in. Carissa's cat, Sweetie, did not welcome Pepper and continuously hissed and growled whenever the "intruder" got close. She was a one-owner cat and only loved Carissa and tolerated those who fed her. The cats learned to get along, but Pepper knew who was boss!

As I reflected over '05 and anticipated what was to come in '06, I continually thanked God for the blessings in my life—my cherished daughters and my extraordinary family and faithful friends. It seems like I'm always asking for help from those around me, from picking up things I drop to repair jobs on my chair, van, or house.

My life lesson 23: To steal a quote from my daily calendar, "To those who matter in our life, time is the most valuable gift we can give. When we give of ourselves, we share the finest gift of all!"

CHAPTER TWENTY-FOUR

A Visit Back Home

Ft. Worth, Texas, 2006

One aspect of the divorce I didn't like was that my ability to travel was limited as Stephen had always helped with the lifting onto the airplane seat or driving the long distances. So it was a big deal when the girls and I decided to make a trip back to Ft. Worth in 2006 to visit with my dear friends from our Koinonia Class and our friends from All Saints Episcopal School. It took me six years to convince myself I would be able to make the drive. Four hours of driving time is easy for most people. For me, it can be exhausting. We only had one mishap where I didn't see the exit for I-35 West, and we got lost for about twenty minutes. I have no sense of direction, even in a shopping mall, so it didn't take much to get turned around. We were driving in circles through some construction sites and kept calling our friends, who we would be staying with, for help on finding our way back to I-35 West. Carissa's godparents, Don and Mary Beth Lampe, hosted a party where we could meet with all our friends at one time. It was wonderful to see everyone after being away six years, and we couldn't have had more gracious hosts than the Lampes.

It was rewarding to watch my girls find their passion in life and growing up to be independent and focused on their goals. At this point in time, Carissa was a senior and working steadily on college applications. She was looking at Baylor, Texas, Christian University and, to my Aggie horror, University of Texas. She was interested in the interior design program and considered making that her major. Cailey was in her final year of middle school and doing every sport, except for basketball—the only sport where her small size was a definite hardship. Where she was small, though, she made up with her aggressiveness and "I can do it" attitude. We discovered one of her hidden talents when she performed with her cousin, Dani, at the Memorial Middle Talent Show. Cailey sang while Dani played the violin to a country song by the Wreckers, "Leave the Pieces." Considering she comes from a tone-deaf mother and grandmother, this was impressive.

I was back to wearing special pressure boots for my feet; otherwise, my health was perfect for a quadriplegic. I'm dangerous; however, when I'm backing up, whether it is in my wheelchair or my van. Remember how I backed over Cailey in my wheelchair when she was just learning to crawl and sneaked up behind me. I continually banged into walls in my house when backing up. And last but not least, my back wheels find coworkers' toes quite frequently. My most puzzling experience this year had been when my wheelchair footrest kept rising of its own accord. Every time I looked down, they would be raised, when I know I had just lowered them. I thought I was going crazy! It was a relief to know it was just a control feature run amok! It finally got resolved, and I rushed back to work where I backed into a stop sign at SAM'S Club. With all the dents it already had, I decided it was time to give myself a Christmas gift of a van makeover. No sooner had the van been repaired and looking like new when my own daughter Carissa backed into my van in our car port. It was my fault, of course, as she explained I was parked in the middle—not anticipating her to return so soon. My New Year's resolution for the year was to avoid denting my car and to try not to run over anyone's toes, with the former one being easier than the latter. I always tried to find a quote to live by each year. It has always helped to keep my positive attitude. For this year, I picked one off the internet, "The happiest of people don't necessarily have the best of everything; they just make the most of everything that comes along their way." I truly related to this quote. I do not get to go on fancy trips or buy luxury items for my family; however, I am blessed with the time I spend with my awesome daughters and wonderful supportive family and coworkers I enjoy, and an awesome God who blesses me every day with adventures—even if they may prove to be a pain in the butt!

My life lesson 24: You don't have to look too far for blessings. Oftentimes, you are surrounded!

CHAPTER TWENTY-FIVE

Upgrade

Houston, 2007

I started off the year 2007 with four burned toes on my left foot from sitting too close to an open fire on New Year's Eve. The danger for people with spinal cord injuries is the fact that we do not have any sensation below the level of our injury and don't feel burns, bruises, or the pain associated that most people would know immediately. I will not know until I get into bed that evening and my caregiver discovers the problem. Never would I have imagined that it would be May before they were officially healed. I had continued to nurse the pressure sore from December of the previous year; and now that it had healed, I scraped the same toes I burned last year! You might say the wound center was a second home. I loved the staff and their hot chocolate. I also found out from one of the doctors who looked at my toes that I'm tetraplegic instead of quadriplegic. I assumed this was an improvement or an upgrade in modern terms, but I'm not quite sure.

I began writing my Christmas letters back in the mid-'80s, never imagining I would have children at that point. I could not believe my two beautiful daughters! Carissa was entering college, and Cailey would be a freshman in high school! Time flies when you're having fun but primarily because you're busy!

Carissa turned eighteen in June and entered Texas Christian University (TCU) in the fall. She was majoring in interior design. She pledged Delta Gamma and was enjoying both TCU and the sorority. My aunt Carolyn Dixon was thrilled that Carissa had chosen TCU (where she also graduated from, taught, and went on to be the director of Women's Athletics). I'm sad to say that in November Carolyn died of a heart attack and Carissa would miss sharing her experiences at TCU with her great-aunt. Carissa still had another great-aunt, Patricia Reed, and great-uncle, Al, who were excited to have her close by and would look forward to her visits out to their farm in Granbury. Carissa was also blessed with having her godparents, Don and Marybeth Lampe, nearby to nurture her as well. Her highlight of 2007 was a generous gift from her best friend, Kelli, and her mom, Kim, taking her on a seven-day cruise to Mexico as a high school graduation gift! I missed having my organized, nurturing daughter at home, but was happy she was thriving at TCU.

Cailey was active in soccer. Her club team went to Ft. Lauderdale, Florida, on December 26 for a tournament. She decided she liked it out there and wanted to move there eventually. Her real interest was in volunteering. The previous summer, she was a zoo volunteer and helped with the kids attending camp. She also worried about the environment and encouraged recycling. Our dinner menus were also vastly different since she had decided that the vegetarian life was best for her. I will always be a pork chop and potato kind of girl.

I was still at SAM'S Club and looking forward to being fully vested in 2008! I appreciated the flexibility they allowed, and the commute was only seven minutes! I was determined to stay until the freeway was completed in front of the club and our store was making a profit. That meant I would probably retire from SAM'S Club! Karen and I attended our Milby High School Reunion, 29 and 30 respectively. Karen treated me to a makeover, and we stayed overnight at the South Shore Harbour Resort where the reunion was held. We were real glamour girls that night. My primary focus for the year, as always, was enjoying my lovely daughters and watching them grow into independent, prospering young women. I wish I could take all the credit; but in truth, we have continually been surrounded by family and friends who bless us throughout the year, both emotionally and financially.

My life lesson 25: Life should not be a journey to the grave with the intention of arriving safely in an attractive and well-preserved body but rather to skid in sideways, chocolate in one hand, wine in the other, body thoroughly used up, totally worn out, and screaming, "Woo-hoo, what a ride!"

I CLIMBED BEFORE
I CRAWLED

Essay by Carissa in Senior Year of High School

I am different from most kids because my mom is quadriplegic. For me, this simply means that she has no feeling or muscle movement from her waist down. Since my mom is paralyzed, it was a lot more difficult for her to raise me, especially when I was learning to walk. One of the things my mom likes to joke about with me is how I learned to climb up to my mom's chair before I even crawled because my mom could not bend over to pick me up. Compared to other children, I was probably raised a little differently since my mom could not do all the things that a normal mom could. I had different responsibilities as a result of my mom's situation.

After my sister and I were born, my mom quit her job to stay with us at home. Every day we would sit in her room and draw pictures of each other or of places we would like to go. She would also write notes to me on my pictures. To this day, I still have a note that she wrote me that said, "Someday I hope I can walk so I will know what it is like to hug you standing up." Simple actions such as this showed me a sincere form of compassion and unconditional love. Indirectly, my mom's condition taught me a lot about self-discipline. I learned a lot earlier than most kids about responsibility since my mom could not clean up after me. I never viewed my responsibilities as chores. I did them to return my love to my mom. I was willing to help in any way. Most of my friends in elementary school thought my mom was cool. They would take turns riding on the back of my mom's electric wheelchair as she zoomed them around. I would get my turn every morning when my dad would come in to wake me up, followed by my mom, who asked me to climb on her chair as she called out, "Wheelchair Express!" and drove me to the breakfast table. Besides my mom's fascinating wheelchair, she also has a van with a ramp so that she can easily get into her car. I always loved watching children's reactions to our specialized vehicle. One time, a kid walked by and said, "Mom! It's a spaceship!" This handicap has always earned us the best parking spaces in parking lots. However, most people don't realize how complicated things get with a ramp. It seemed that whenever we were in the biggest hurry, someone would park next to my mom's van, blocking the area where her ramp needed to come down. I will never forget how I felt when my mom, out of desperation, first asked me to back her car out of a parking space when I was only eleven years old. With no one else around, I was forced to quickly maneuver the car out of the parking spot while standing up, since the driver's seat had been removed to fit my mom's chair at the wheel.

Because of my mom's condition I have also learned to do things in non-conventional ways. For example, since my mom does not have the use of the muscles in her hands, she would pull on my socks and shoes with her teeth. Most children learn by watching the way their parents raise them, so after observing my mom dress me in this way, I thought that was how I should do it. My mom walked in on me one morning as I was attempting to put on my socks with my teeth and asked me what I was doing. She had failed to mention that her way was a "special way" to put on socks and shoes, and that I could use my hands. As I continued to grow, I attained my knowledge from a different perspective because of my mom's circumstance.

I often think about what must have gone through my mom's head when the doctors first told her that she would never walk again. When I think about my mom in this way, I realize how truly spectacular and strong she is. She has always kept a positive attitude while most other people might have turned their backs on life. This has taught me to never think negatively about things. My best qualities come from my mom. While most other parents put pressure on their kids to make perfect grades, my mom never put pressure on me because she always knew I would automatically do my best without her ever having to ask me to. Out of the people in my life, my mom has had the greatest impact on me and has left me with knowledge and experience that has matured me beyond my years.

CHAPTER TWENTY-SIX

Rocking and Rolling at Fifty

Houston, 2008

We had a great '08. Fortunately, it was an uneventful year—no burned toes, no wrecks, and no crazy wheelchair stunts. Well, maybe one. I was blessed with a new wheelchair (Texas Aggie maroon with matching maroon hub caps!) in August. Thanks to the generosity of the Texas Department of Rehabilitation Services (DARS), I was fortunate to have Pham and Katherine of DARS to guide me through the process and provide both the new wheelchair and a shower chair. Only a few months later, this brand-new wheelchair would not go forward. It was déjà vu, as this same thing had occurred several years earlier in Ft. Worth. It was inconvenient but easily resolved with new ball bearings. I celebrated my fiftieth birthday that year. It was a milestone as it marked twenty-five years walking and twenty-five years rolling! My family and friends helped me celebrate at Karen's beautiful newly renovated house. My birthday invitation stated,

25 Years Rocking, 25 Years Rolling
At 25 years I had a wreck
At 50, I say, "What the Heck!"
I got to rock for half my life
Now I roll with challenges & strife.
I praise our Lord I'm healthy and hearty
Please no gifts just help me party!

Carissa was a sophomore at TCU. She continued to enjoy her sorority, Delta Gamma. A sorority sister, Maddie, invited her to South Padre on her fall break. I'm grateful she had this opportunity as it's something I could not afford. She worked part-time for the University Phon-a-Thon, calling for donations to keep tuition cost down. She was promoted to a marketing specialist. Her major changed from interior design to advertising and public relations, so she was less stressed with all night projects and eager to see where this path led. She contemplated starting a business that summer where she would organize people's closets, pantries, etc. You wouldn't believe what Carissa could do with a messy room or closet. She had lots of practice with her sister's room.

Cailey was a sophomore at Memorial High School. She turned sixteen in October but had shown no desire to get a driver's license. Her attitude was "If I don't have a car, why do I need a license?" It worked for me since it delayed an increase in my insurance! She had changed her hair color to red, which fit her personality. You could spot her on the soccer field now. She continued with Albion Soccer and JV Soccer at Memorial High School. Cailey's new interest was in theater arts. She was a natural-born performer and fit right in. That summer, she hoped to raise enough money to go on a trip to Costa Rica on a community service project, combined with adventure and fun. She went to Florida for a soccer tournament with Albion. Unfortunately, she had been sick when everyone left and didn't make the carpool. Saturday morning, I got an urgent call asking if Cailey could get to the tournament. She decided she could go, so we raced to the airport. Cailey was the only walk-on that made the flight to Florida. Our experiences in the airport haven't always been that lucky. I remember one Christmas had us stuck overnight with the girls sleeping on the floor and me in my wheelchair.

My favorite soccer action shot of Cailey

My life lesson 26: Whether you are rocking or rolling, celebrate your life every day like a party.

CHAPTER TWENTY-SEVEN

The Arrival of My Angel

Austin, Texas, 2009

We made two trips that year. One was to Austin, for my interview to be considered for an assistance dog from the Texas Hearing and Service Dogs (name later changed to Service Dogs Inc.). Cailey said her back was already hurting from always picking up things for me. Hopefully, I wouldn't get so many complaints from my dog! Our second trip was to Galveston (before Hurricane Ike) for fun and relaxation. There would be a lot of unknowns in the coming year, but one thing never changed. I was so blessed with wonderful family and friends; good health (despite being over the hill); and loving, thoughtful daughters.

In August of 2009, my mom went with me for my week-long training for Angel—soon to be my service dog—in Dripping Springs, twenty miles outside Austin, Texas. We stayed in Extended Stay America, where the rates were lower because your room was not cleaned daily, as in other hotels. I did not know this when I made my arrangements, so if my mother had not been with me, it would have been much more challenging if not impossible. She helped with bed changes and maintained clean towels as well as prepared meals for my lunch and our dinner together when I returned each afternoon. I would need to be at Texas Hearing and Service Dogs (THSD) by 8:30 a.m. and return by 4:00 p.m. to the hotel. We also arranged for a home health service to help with my personal care. We only had one mishap with the aide dropping me on the floor; but overall, it was positive and provided much help to my mom, who would not have been able to handle my caregiving alone. Everyone at THSD was wonderful to work with. Throughout the week, I got to know the trainers and the other clients receiving service dogs. It was exhausting having to fit all their expertise into five days! Not only do they work with a client for that week; my trainer, Susan, came once a week for three months to continue working with Angel and me at home. I can't say enough about THSD. They provided the biggest blessing of a dog I could ever hope for. It cost $17,500 per dog to train, and all they asked of the client was a $25 (now $50) application fee and fund raise $100 per year. I have not been good about the fundraising since I am not comfortable asking people for money, but I plan to give proceeds from this book to THSD for my ten-plus years with Angel. My quote for this year was, "Don't tell the Lord how big the problem is. Tell the problem how great the Lord is!"

When Angel came into our household, one pet, Sweetie (Carissa's cat), was not thrilled to welcome Angel. She had been the "queen" for eleven years and did everything possible to scare Angel into leaving. This cat would get in Angel's face and strike her face with her clawless paws. Another trick was to jump out at her as she walked down the hall and again thrust her paws at her nose. Angel was convinced and avoided Sweetie by turning the opposite direction whenever she was in her path. My trainer, Susan, said it was better to have the dog beware of the cat instead of the other way around. Our other cat, Pepper, could take her or leave her and he was the one who could be a serious threat with his claws. Sweetie died following Carissa's college graduation, so Angel felt more secure in her home and had begun a guarded friendship with Pepper. You might wonder how I manage the care of the animals. I have for years had to clean up poop from the cats, and sometimes even vomit. I use my Reacher—basically a large tweezer. I hold a paper towel with the Reacher to pick it up the poop and put it on some foil. I can then roll up the foil and dispose of the foul substance. The girls gave me an elevated tray that houses two bowls for food and water. This allowed me to feed Angel without having to bend over to the floor.

In 2010, Angel had been with me for more than a year now and had become like a sidecar to my wheelchair. She went just about everywhere and attracted attention with her dreamy "love me" eyes. She made a great companion as she looked at me constantly for what to do or what treats she was going to get for doing it. She was even very forgiving when I accidentally ran over her! Our excitement for the year was meeting "the Fonz," a.k.a. Henry Winkler, at an Abilities Exposition. We were there representing Texas Hearing and Service Dogs. Angel performed during a demonstration, showing the types of things she did for me. My favorite was when she pulled clothes out of the washer and dryer, with a little growl for effect. She also groaned when she didn't get her way. In April, I celebrated having been with Sam's Club for ten years. Angel fit right in and barked along with all the employees who cheered at our morning meetings.

I had spent half of the year, once again, at the wound center. This time, I was not sure of the cause. It was believed to be a spider bite; whatever it was, it had not healed and had challenged the Katy Wound Center since July. I had a procedure, a skin graft, the last week of December to, hopefully, heal the wound. It frightened me when they decided I had to be put "under" with anesthesia. My doctor had previously said it could be done with a local sedation. I believe I was told years ago in rehabilitation; it was dangerous to receive anesthesia because my blood pressure remains so low. My typical blood pressure was 75/40, sometimes even 67/40. When I'm at any doctor's office, I can always predict the nurse will check and recheck my blood pressure with a puzzled look on his or her face— not believing it could be that low. I had one doctor at a rehab facility comment, "I know you're sitting here talking to me. I'm just not sure how!" Carissa had gone with me for my support system. I thought I would have a local sedative and be done a few hours later. As it turned out, I got weepy with Carissa, worried I may not wake up after the surgery, even though the anesthesiologist assured me she would keep it under control. So Carissa called in her support system, my sister Karen, in case something did go wrong. Well, all my worry was silly as I made it through the skin graft just fine and drove myself home once the anesthesia was cleared of my system.

My life lesson 27: Blessings come in all forms.

Angel in My Life

Often, I think Angel is my dad reincarnated. She just has this way she looks at me that makes me feel I'm being watched over. Of course, she gazes at everyone with the "I love you. Do you love me?" look.

Before Angel, I spent a lot of time leaning over in my wheelchair retrieving things—many times to the point of tears.

The times I do hold a pity party are when I'm by myself and cannot accomplish a task or drop food on the floor and must call for help. I once dropped fried chicken from my refrigerator and had to call upon a neighbor to pick it up

The hardest part has always been constantly asking others for help. Angel has cut down on most calls, except for the dropped food, obviously.

Angel has also become a big help to me in the laundry department. She will help tug items—mainly towels or sheets—from the washing machine or dryer. This is one of her favorite tasks, as she gets a treat after each item. If she could fold them, it would be great, but then I would probably lose her to worldwide fame.

As with my children when they were in diapers, cleaning up her poop is an act of love!

A child once asked me if the dog was walking me.

Karen and my daughters think Angel just may start talking because she seems so human.

I get a kick out of people who ask if I'm blind because I have a service dog at my side, also, the people who want to pray over me. A woman saw me drive up to the Social Security office and, assuming Angel was a seeing-eye dog, asked if I was blind. I was so stunned I wasn't sure how to respond. She then went on to say, "If I wasn't blind, what did she do for me?"

Upon completion of my book, Angel was in the final stages of her life. What I will always treasure about her is the way she looks at me. A photographer captured it accurately recently, and I've included the photo. The only way I can describe it is human and soulful. I will go through the process of training with another dog though Service Dogs Inc. But no relationship will compare with this one I've had for ten and a half years with my dear Angel.

CHAPTER TWENTY-EIGHT

Everything That Could Go Wrong, Did!

Houston to Ft. Worth, 2011

Carissa graduated from Texas Christian University in May 2011! You just would not believe what happened along the way to the ceremony (or maybe you would after hearing all my transportation struggles). I really felt there was a conspiracy to keep Cailey, my mom, and me from attending because so many obstacles cropped up at every turn. Cailey, who had just gotten her driver's license in April and had very little freeway experience, drove like a pro, despite the stress of two backseat drivers in her midst. Suffice it to say, everything that could break down did. We made it within two to three minutes of Carissa walking across the stage to receive her diploma. It's impossible to appreciate everything that occurred without a time line of the day:

- 7:00 a.m.—my caregiver, Sol, discovered a water leak under my van and added a gallon of water to my radiator.
- 7:15 a.m.—we stopped at the Shell station and discovered the radiator was cracked and should not be driven. The Shell station owner said he would not have anyone in until 8:30 a.m. to start repair.
- 7:30 a.m.—we arrived at Firestone and pleaded my case, explaining we were trying to get to daughter's college graduation in Ft. Worth by 3:00 p.m. They said they would look at it and do the best they could do. A technician did not get to my van until after 8:00 a.m. Once they had it up on the rack, they came and explained it was not just the

radiator that was cracked, it was much worse! He asked if I'd had some work done recently on the shocks because the job had not been done properly. A pin was broken and hanging—causing further difficulty—and would take at least six hours to repair.

- 8:30 a.m.—Bob walked in because my mom had called big brother to the rescue. He spoke to the mechanic and saw the problem. We called Carissa and Mimi to update them on our situation. Mimi said she had almost lost faith, that this just wasn't fair. Carissa just wanted us to get on the road! I spoke to Bob about using his mother-in-law's, Pat's, van as it was also equipped with a ramp. He called Pat and came back ten minutes later recommending we not use her van because it had not been driven much and there was no telling what kind of problems it might have.

- 9:00 a.m.—Bob came back to Firestone in Pat's van to transport Cailey and me back to our house. We discussed renting a car but discovered we could not because Cailey, the designated driver at that point, was not eligible, since the driver must be at least twenty-one years old.

- 9:15 a.m.—Bob and Cailey worked on putting air in my manual wheelchair tires while I called rental agencies. The next thing I heard was a loud explosion as my tires exploded from too much inflation. I called Carissa to see if someone in Ft. Worth could pick up tubes for my tires. Don Lampe, her godfather, did better than that; he rented a wheelchair which would be at the graduation when we got there.

- 10:00 a.m.—Bob took Cailey back over to Firestone to retrieve our bags since she figured out to take the Ford Focus, sitting in front of our house. It had just been dropped off by Richard's (Carissa's boyfriend) mom on Wednesday. His parents were leaving for Australia and had gifted the car to Carissa. However, the keys to the Focus were in my van since I was taking them to Carissa. So off they went to get the luggage and keys, only returning five minutes later to say Pat's car had ironically overheated! Bob had predicted correctly about not taking that van.

- 10:30 a.m.—Dani, Cailey's cousin, came to get Cailey in her dad's truck to get our belongings before the van went up on the rack for repair.
- 10:50 a.m.—Dani and Cailey got back and transferred our luggage to the Ford Focus. Ironically, the manual wheelchair would not have fit into the car, so the blown tires did not matter at this point.
- 11:00 a.m.—Bob transferred me from my motorized wheelchair to the front passenger seat of Focus. He then drove my motorized wheelchair back into the house, and we got on the road.
- 11:05 a.m.—Cailey noticed a red light that was on and asked me about it. It didn't occur to me to check the emergency brake.
- 11:10 a.m.—we were driving toward the freeway frontage road to get on the freeway when we smelled something burning! We decided to go back to Firestone, and along the way, someone in the car next to us at the light was trying to tell us our tires were smoking! Cailey had to lean over me to roll down the manual window to communicate with the concerned driver.
- 11:20 a.m.—we got to the Firestone where we were well-known by then and have them check the tires and emergency brake now that we had driven with it on for several miles. Meanwhile, Carissa kept texting us just to drive! I texted back we were not getting on the road until I knew it was safe.
- 11:45 a.m.—we were cleared to leave and finally got on the road.
- 12:40 p.m.—we stopped in Navasota and picked up Mimi, who had parked her car at a location on the bypass, to make it more convenient. We loaded her luggage into the Ford Focus and kept on going.
- 1:00 p.m.—we stopped in College Station for gas.

- 3:00 p.m.—we were in Waco, texting back and forth with Carissa and Don Lampe (waiting with a wheelchair) on our status.
- 3:45 p.m.—we got to the colosseum and rode around looking for the correct entrance three times before getting it right and spotting Don with the wheelchair. Don transferred me from the car to the wheelchair and literally raced with me through the building. He parked me in the handicap seating area—just as they were reading the last names with *As* in Carissa's college. We saw Carissa cross the stage for her diploma about two to three minutes later! Cailey said once Carissa saw I was there that she had a definite skip to her walk and was obviously pleased we got there in time.
- 6:00 p.m.—we celebrated her graduation at the Lampe's wonderful home.

Sunday

- 10: a.m.—I spun around in the manual chair when I was trying to lean over to fix my footing. I'm always picky about little things, and it almost caused me to fall out of the wheelchair, if Cailey had not grabbed the chair to settle it.
- 12:00 p.m.—we were on the road again, back home—fortunately at a slower pace.

Carissa had several internships with prestigious public relations firms, which led to great opportunities after she graduated. She moved off campus into a house with three roommates that year and picked up a newfound hobby of cooking. Every time she came home, she cooked something new for us and left lots of food for us to enjoy. Even though I was hoping Carissa would find employment in Houston and be close, I am proud she got a job so soon out of college and stayed in Ft. Worth. She was hired by Consuro Managed Technology, as their marketing coordinator. My mind boggled at the thought of her responsibilities, but she was adjusting beautifully to the "outside" world with much poise and maturity. She also continued cooking and had created a blog called "Alice in Cooking land," playing on her middle name, Alice.

In June, Carissa was invited by Richard and his parents to go to Scotland. It was an exciting trip because she visited another country for the first time and got to meet Richard's relatives. She would not have had this opportunity without their generosity.

My life lesson 28: When life throws you obstacles, play dodgeball with all you have at your fingertips!

CHAPTER TWENTY-NINE

From Essays to Dolphins

Houston, 2011

Cailey graduated from Memorial High School in May 2011! She was chosen all-region soccer forward and made academic all-district. She had applied to schools from Maine to California, everywhere except Texas; so it was a forgone conclusion that she would leave for parts unknown. The most amazing news was regarding a scholarship she had applied for in the spring. Discover called her to inform her that she was the recipient of a $40,000 scholarship because of her essay on demonstrating accomplishments in community service and leadership while facing significant roadblocks and challenges. She was also rewarded several other generous scholarships (I believe her essay called "Little Helper" helped a lot) from the George and Mary Josephine Hamman Foundation, Houston Works USA from the city of Houston, and the Houston Zoo. She was accepted into the University of California at Berkley. Cailey decided to take matters in her own hand and started Berkley in July so that she could obtain in-state tuition on her own behalf. That was my enterprising Cailey.

She was relieved not to have to write any more college essays. She absolutely loved her internship in the Bahamas the previous August, and we owed so much of that opportunity to her aunt Karen, who chaperoned and covered more than half of the expenses. It was a once-in-a-lifetime opportunity, which gave her an edge on her résumé. She worked closely with the dolphin trainers and received hands-on experience with marine life.

We had been very blessed in 2010. I still could not believe that Carissa graduated in May from college and Cailey from high school! When we moved to Houston in May 2000 (Carissa in sixth grade and Cailey in second), this milestone seemed a lifetime away. In what seemed like a blink of the eye, it had arrived!

I spent Christmas in the hospital! I had tried desperately to stay out of it by having the antibiotic needed for my infection done intravenously at home; however, by Wednesday of that Christmas week, it was evident that I was destined to be put in the hospital and not to get out until Sunday after the holiday.

My life lessons 29: Appreciate every moment with your children before they become adults. It does seem to pass "in the blink of an eye."

LITTLE HELPER

Cailey's College Essay, 2011

There is a photograph of me in the *Fort Worth Star Telegram* newspaper when I was only two years old. I sat upon my mother's lap and was reaching up to get produce in a grocery store for my mother, who is in a wheelchair. My mother has been disabled for half of her life. She was in a car accident when she was 25 years of age, in which her car rolled down a 30-foot ravine while she was ejected out of the car window and out onto the frozen ground of Grandview, Texas. It was winter, and she was traveling to visit my Mimi for Christmas. She survived and went on to have two miracles after she became paralyzed. I am one of her miracles and I have been her "little helper" since I could walk. It is what has made me the independent and spirited individual I am today.

My mother has always depended on me to help her and help myself. Many people do not understand the amount of hardships that are placed on people that are paralyzed. Obviously, there are the overwhelming aspects of being paralyzed, for instance, not being able to walk or not able to rise out of bed by themselves. However, there are also the small aspects like not being able to pick up a pen to write a quick note or dropping a fork and having to obtain your "Reacher" to pick the fork up again. Or maybe when you are trying to find a parking space, and all the handicaps spots are taken with SUVs with little blue tags you must search for another parking spot for twenty minutes. I always joked with my mother that, "They pass those little blue tags out like candy!" These examples are just a few of the many things my mother goes through every day and has needed my assistance on daily basis. I must admit that many times I have resented the fact that I must "help" her so much; however, I appreciate the many lessons and opportunities that have arisen from these responsibilities.

My mother's dependence on me has taught me to put others in front of myself. This trait has developed my love of helping others through volunteering. Volunteering at the Houston Zoo has facilitated me in finding my one true passion in life which is working with animals. At times, I do doubt and ask myself, "Am I really capable of achieving my goals?" My mother always said, "Never be afraid of going after what you want no matter how many people say that you can't do it." Those words have given me the inspiration to follow my dreams. You could say that my mother has aided in my coming of life, as well as my reason for life.

Having my mother depend on me has also given me the strength of perseverance. I have learned this trait by observing my mom over the past years. For instance, one day I was in my room watching TV. I had been hearing a groaning noise for about ten minutes. I decided to get up and see what the noise was. As I entered the room, I see my mom, halfway under the desk, reaching for something. "What's going on?" I asked my mom. "Ugh!" she groans, "I dropped my pencil!" My mom had been reaching for a pencil for about ten minutes. It is hard for me to imagine having to bend over backwards for ten minutes for such an insignificant object. Small events such as these, gave me the strength of persevering everything.

Some people may look at my mother, my sister and my situation and feel sorry for us; however, the situation gave us more gifts than discord. The situation has bonded us together as a family. It has given me the valuable life-lesson of finding my own self. My mother's circumstance has given me the gift of what life is about, and now it is dependent upon me to carry out this gift and use it to the best of my ability.

CHAPTER THIRTY

The Empty Nest

Houston, 2012

Angel and I were finally adjusting to "our" empty nest. I believe it was just as hard on her as it was for me to see it happen. She looked forward to the occasional weekends when Carissa could come home and take her on a good run. Although I had the benefit of keeping up with the girls on "Skype," Angel didn't respond to their usual squeals at getting her attention. She continued to command attention with her "dreamy" eyes. The most rewarding part of having a service dog, other than the obvious benefits, was the fact people approach me and strike up a conversation, whereas, they probably would not without her. Angel has been a blessing, no doubt about it!

I was still going to the Katy Wound Center for a twenty-eight round trip to medically treat the bug bite from last year. This involved a skin grafts surgery (a skin flap taken from my upper leg to cover the wound on my lower leg), ten weeks of hyperbaric chamber treatments, and several synthetic skin grafts. My wound was finally healed with Ultrasonic Mist Therapy at the Northwest Medical Center (which I drove fifty-four miles round trip generally three times per week). At home, my wonderful caregivers were instrumental in keeping proper ointments on my wounds. After two years and $100,000 plus spent, the insurance company must have been wondering how many legs I have! My thought then was that I might even get my book written before my wounds healed! I do want to comment here how much I appreciated everyone at both wound centers. When you spend as much time as I have with these nurses, doctors, and therapists, they became like family.

What I have always valued most in life is my relationship with both my daughters. Carissa gave me a beautiful picture frame for Christmas, and in it, she had made a large letter C to the power of 3 (C^3). All our names start with the letter C, and it has been just the three of us since 2000. It remains proudly displayed in my den as a reminder of our strong bond.

Carissa always remembered the pictures we would draw and/or color together. She probably liked the fact her pictures would normally be better than mine. I can only draw trees, flowers, the sun, and the moon decently; but it always seemed to make her happy. Cailey liked to recall our special moments in the car when we rocked along with the music. I probably looked as silly as I felt when I shook my head and rotated my shoulders, and we won't even discuss my singing voice. I was told by Carissa when she was a young child, when I was attempting a lullaby, "You don't need to sing, Mommy." Cailey expressed the same sentiment as a teenager when I would sing along with the radio.

It had been tough since both girls were gone except for weekends or holidays. I had adjusted to the quiet house but welcomed their chatter, laughter, and even Cailey's mess when they returned home. The only crazy thing that had occurred to remind me of my helplessness was while alone in bed one night, discovering a bat flying in circles above my head at 3:00 a.m. I knew I would never get back to sleep for the rest of the night with that intruder in my house; so I called my tenant, Victoria, who lived in my garage apartment to come save me. Fortunately, since she answered on the second ring, I did not believe I woke her up. She was over in a New York minute to see what the problem was. Unfortunately, the bat chose that time to hibernate somewhere, and she never saw it—and left. I searched the house the next morning and closed each door as I inspected it for the bat's presence. I thought maybe it would just die eventually with no food or water. Two days later, I was awakened again by the bat circling around my ceiling. Angel jumped up on my bed, equally alarmed by our intruder, and nudged her head against my stomach like I could protect her. Once again, I called Victoria to come over in the wee hours of the morning. I'd like to, at this point, brag on what an understanding tenant she was. This time, she came over armed with a flashlight and broom and saw the bat as soon as she entered the house. I was grateful I wasn't crazy after all. I was beginning to think maybe I was dreaming beforehand. In a few minutes, I heard the pounding of the broom and was rewarded when she showed me the dead bat which would no longer disturb my sleep. Sorry to any animal lovers, but I didn't know of any other way to get rid of the flying menace. I was looking out for myself.

Sounds crazy, but what I wished for was little goals. Instead of walking, I'd be content to be able to wear shoes again. Heck, they did not have to even be fashionable. When I enviously observe people trying on shoes, I remind myself that it could be worse and I could have no feet!

When I see people staring at other people with disabilities, I'm torn between making a face or smiling, but smiling normally wins out. Smiling is like the phrase "A picture is worth a thousand words." Similarly, smiles express more emotions, i.e., "Hi there," "Welcome," "Glad to see you," etc. I experienced a baffling moment at SAM'S Club when I was coming off the elevator to get my water jug filled. A woman was standing in front of the water fountain, so I was waiting for her to move, and she looked at me and said, "I have no money," I guess thinking I was looking for a handout. That was a first for me. I didn't even know how to respond to that insult.

The latest event added to "Pain in Butt" category was when I took my car to SAM'S Club where I worked, to get a tire changed. I had been having a problem with my car vibrating when I got up to sixty miles per hour. My brother Bob had said it was a tire-balance issue; however, I had already had this service performed three times. Recently, SAM'S Club had told me it was an alignment problem. So during the weekend of Cailey's last weekend at home before going back to Berkeley, I spent three hours at one shop having my power lock-in on the van repaired and then stopping at another shop to have the alignment looked at. Carissa was coming in from Ft. Worth to surprise Cailey on her last weekend. We had led her to believe she wasn't able to make it. Cailey was excited at Carissa's arrival. I barely beat Carissa home from the alignment shop to join in the event. The next morning, after spending $665 for the alignment, the girls and I left for my mom's place in Navasota. To my disappointment, the car still shook! The alignment manager said it would not stop shaking until I replaced the bad tire on the driver's side. So on Sunday, I was back at SAM'S Club to get the tire replaced. I was in the store for about twenty minutes when I heard my name being paged to the membership desk. I thought they had finished with my van. On the contrary, Ana Lila, my evening caregiver, who also worked at SAM'S Club, was telling me I needed to get over to the tire department because they had crashed my van! Sure enough, when I went around the building with my heart beating harder with every second, I came upon several tire department associates and two managers looking at the right front end of my car. The awful evidence was staring right back at me. All I could think of was, "Sure it could be repaired, but that's not the real problem for me. For me, it's the inconvenience of not having it while it is in for repair." The following day, both SAM'S Club Management and the Claims Department attempted to locate a rental van for a person with a disability. I could have told them it was impossible with my specific requirements; however, they were determined to try. Later, they discovered what I already knew—the only van found was one with manual tie-downs in the driver seat. I appreciated their enthusiasm to try to help me, offering to show up each morning to lock me in, unlock me at SAM'S Club, and then do the reverse when it was time for me to go home. This was way too much trouble, and even though I knew it was going to be inconvenient for me, I offered to ride the bus for people with disabilities called Metro Lift. After riding the bus one week, I wished I could have put the inconvenience back on them! It's tough when you are used to independence and then must give it up, even temporarily.

My life lesson 30: Something I have learned from my disability is that I'm never alone. God has continually directed me to look for the blessings in every person and situation around me.

CHAPTER THIRTY-ONE

Learning to Do Things Differently

Berkeley, California, 2012

In October of 2012, in conjunction with Cailey's birthday, we visited her in Berkeley. Carissa drove from Ft. Worth and got on the airplane along with Angel and me at Houston Hobby Airport. Angel had no problem adjusting to the flight; she jumped right into the seat between us and remained there the entire trip. The attendants said it was okay and were charmed by her sweet eyes, as were the passengers passing by our seats. It was all a new experience for us all when we arrived in California and rode the BART (Bay Area Rapid Transit) from Oakland to downtown Berkeley. It was wonderful to be reunited after five months—the longest she had ever been away. We were there for five days and spent one day touring around San Francisco. The rest of our time was spent exploring the Berkeley campus and appreciating what college life was like for Cailey in those beautiful hills! Angel got used to the bus rides but never really felt comfortable on the BART. We also got to visit with Carissa's boyfriend (now husband), Richard, who had been accepted into the Culinary Institute of America at Napa Valley in August. He was a good sport when my wheelchair battery needed to be recharged, and he had to cart the heavy charger in his backpack up a hill to Cailey's dorm.

It was a big event for us since I had not taken a trip of this magnitude since my divorce. The girls were both helpful in making it a success. I am so blessed to have these two beautiful, adoring daughters in my life to remind me of God's abundant love, despite my difficult circumstances.

I do not want to close my book without describing our latest major event at the Trois Eperon Ranch—Carissa and Richard's wedding. In her usual fashion, Carissa organized the entire weekend using a four-page color-coded spreadsheet! The most fun were the dances. Carissa choreographed our dance to Bruno Mars's song "Uptown Funk." The girls asked me if I heard all the screaming and clapping in the background. I didn't. I was concentrating so hard on getting all my moves right. Richard and his mom did a Scottish jig. Fortunately, the only glitch in the event was getting me out of the bus (which Carissa had arranged for to bring all the guests out to the ranch) where I was stuck for about ten to fifteen minutes. The wedding could not start without me as I was "walking" her down the drive to Richard. A big difference between my wedding and theirs was in the videotaping. My grandfather, who was around eighty at the time, taped my wedding with the camera upside down! These were my last recorded steps. Carissa had a professional videographer who used drones and several assistants at the wedding who caught everything. They created a wonderful four-minute production (YouTube® "Scotland Meets Texas: A Wedding with Kilts and Cowboy Hats") capturing all of it in a nutshell.

My life lesson 31: Instead of bemoaning the loss of your comfort, accept the challenge of something new. I lead you on from glory to glory making you fit for my kingdom (Jesus Calling Devotional).

Carissa, Cherie, and Cailey dancing at Carissa
and Richard's wedding, April 2016

Cailey, Carissa, and Cherie (C3)

CHAPTER THIRTY-TWO

Surviving the Loss of My Mom

College Station, 2013–2017

Since I said at the beginning that this book was in memory of my mom, it's appropriate that I conclude with my feelings about my loss of this incredible mother. In many ways, it was more difficult to watch my mom with dementia fade away than to handle my physical disability. One of my biggest regrets was not getting her comments about how she felt when I had my accident. My mom developed dementia before she died in 2017, two days after the birth of my first grandson, Connor. My mother was vivacious and never met a stranger. She was not afraid to speak her opinion, especially on politics. She volunteered for former president George Bush when he was running for senator, supported him with her whole heart, and would not let anyone disparage his name in her presence. She was a docent at the George Bush library for twenty years. She never remarried after my father's death in 1992. In her mind, no one could replace my dad.

I was living in Houston in 2013 when we discovered my mom had suffered an episode which we believe was a minor stroke at the ranch. It was when she was in her usual element, outside trying to eliminate an armadillo! Karen had already moved to College Station and was doing what she could to help her. That's when I decided to make the move in November 2013 and help, as well.

One thing you need to understand about my mom is she sacrificed her own comfort and needs to provide for me once I had my divorce. She purchased the house we moved to in Houston following my divorce. It was a beautiful home in a great school district, so the girls could receive the best possible education. It turned out to be a wonderful investment which in turn she used to buy my home in College Station. I believe she knew I appreciated everything she did for me because I often thanked her for her generosity. The best way I could repay my mom's kindness and sacrifice was to live by her example. Although I live on a budget because of my disability, and not knowing what the future holds, I strive to give back to the community with my service and or money when available.

This was a chance to give back to my mom all she had done for me. I'm the first person to admit I don't like change; and moving to College Station meant giving up my church, job, and friends I had developed relationships with for thirteen years. It was déjà vu again, from the time when I had to leave behind a great church and friendships in Ft. Worth after my divorce.

When I first moved to College Station, the townhome I moved into was one Karen and Tom had renovated for my needs. The critical parts of my bedroom and expanded bathroom were completed and good for move in. With this move, I became more independent via more accessibility to closet space, front load laundry, and kitchen appliances. They designed the bathroom and kitchen cabinets with a margin of space below the sinks for my destructive wheelchair maneuvering and with more cabinets I could reach by myself. People who can take care of these things with no effort cannot appreciate the excitement I felt in doing it myself for the first time.

One of my first priorities was to find the right church and start searching for a job. In the first, I was successful, the latter, not so much. I'm not sure if it was due to my disability or my age or a little of both, but I never was able to find a job. Church was a different matter. I visited about four to five churches before I discovered First United Methodist Church in Bryan, which I knew immediately was the right church for me. It became central to my activities in College Station. My minister had preached one Sunday on stepping outside the boat. I had felt compelled to become a Stephen Minister (a one-on-one visitation geared to listening and praying with individuals in need) for years but had been fearful; but my pastor's sermon convinced me to step out and become more involved. It required fifty hours of training and was beneficial to my role as a lay shepherd in my church.

That was followed by my participation in a group called Aggieland Pets with a Purpose. Angel became a therapy dog as well as my service dog. We go around and visit schools and nursing/retirement facilities to relieve people's loneliness. My sister says that I'm the busiest nonworking person she knows.

You might wonder how a quadriplegic could possibly help her aging mom with dementia. I'm sure it was a sight to see because I managed to get my mom into the front seat of my van, take her walker around and put it in my trunk, as well as get Angel in the car. We would make weekly trips to Chick-fil-A or Burger King, her favorite fast-food restaurants. The only time it was difficult was in the Texas heat!

The tough part was getting my mom agreeable to moving from her ranch in Anderson to an independent living facility in College Station, which would be more convenient for us helping her daily. Watercrest served my mom's needs until she began wandering the halls and looking for ways to leave. Fortunately, somebody would find her before that happened. Along with the memory loss, people with dementia often fall, which further debilitates them. I felt so helpless when she fell at my place twice, one time more severe when she hit her head getting out of my van and falling to the ground. It seemed like it took forever for the bleeding to stop!

As I drove my mom to Austin for my niece's wedding, she must have commented on how big Texas was at least seven times and then questioned where we were going. Another result of dementia is their childlike attitudes or expressions. It's almost a role reversal. Regardless, I cherished every moment I had while she was cognitive of who I was—her daughter who loved her dearly. As she deteriorated further, we moved her to an apartment with her own caregiver. She enjoyed the moments when I took her out for lunch or activities. However, once she got to the point she couldn't walk and was also in a wheelchair, I couldn't take her out anymore.

Once my mom was bedridden, she lost the desire to live. It was only a matter of months that I watched my mom deteriorate further and lose the will to fight for life. In a heartwarming moment, my daughter Carissa, who was due to give birth within days, told her Mimi how much she loved her and that she was the woman she was because of her influence. We saw one of her rare smiles at that moment. When Connor was born a week later, I told Mom, her great-grandson Connor arrived safely and had her feisty attitude; and I witnessed one of her last big grins! This vibrant, loving mother at eighty-seven died peacefully and free of dementia which robbed her of memories the last five to six years of her life.

I participate in the Alzheimer's Walk, in memory of Marty Dixon. My mom made me the woman I have become. From her example, I've learned to persevere despite life's challenges and normally with a smile!

"Growing old is hell," my mom said. She hated losing momentum and was such a vibrant active woman that it killed her to slow down, especially once the dementia set in. I have also dealt with aging issues. When I began writing my Christmas letters, I was twenty-six. At the completion of my book I'm 63. However, I don't feel it. I still feel like I'm in my forties. The big difference is my bones don't agree! A big party was planned in downtown Bryan to celebrate my sixtieth birthday. On the Wednesday before my big day, a nurse was on a scheduled visit to change my Foley catheter. The way this had always been done was for me to lie back in my wheelchair. I lift one leg and hold it while the nurse performs the catheterization. I'm not sure exactly why, but the nurse shoved on my raised leg, maybe to get a better view, when suddenly I heard a huge pop and knew something wasn't right. The nurse assured me if something was wrong it would swell. This did not prove to be the case, for when I had it x-rayed the following day, it turned out that my femur was broken! I was put into a leg extension which kept the leg stable until the doctor could do surgery a week later. Fortunately, my wheelchair footrest could be raised, and I could drive my van with the leg raised up. More importantly, I didn't even miss my party!

Two years later, I didn't realize my ankle was turned outward and rolled up against my bed, which broke my tibia and fibula on the same leg! Obviously, I need to slow down because my body is not as young as I think it is. I doubt I'll live into my eighties, because of the issues with spinal cord injuries; but I am sure I will, like my mom, hate slowing down. I now have a two-year-old grandson and a granddaughter on the way to keep me young!

Mom and Cherie in 2016 at Trois Eperon Ranch

My life lesson 32: "Perseverance must finish its work so that you may be mature and complete, not lacking anything" (James 1:4).

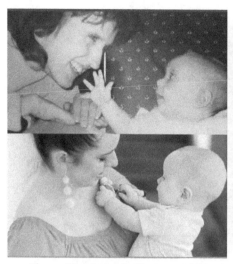

Above Cherie with Carissa, 1989
Below Carissa with my first
grandchild, Connor, 2017

Proud GiGi

Great support system! Annual family Christmas, 2019

Back from left to right: John and Siobhan Dagleish, Ian
Fagerstrom, Sam Hughes, Bob and JoElla Dixon, Mindy and
Clay Dixon with first great-grandchild, Emmalee Jane Dixon
Front from left to right: Richard and Carissa Dagleish
with second great-grandchild, Connor, Cherie

AFTERWORD

Now to him who is able to do immeasurably more than all we ask or imagine, according to his power that is at work within us, to him be glory in the church and in Jesus Christ throughout all generations for ever and ever! Amen.(Ephesians3:20-21)

All my life, I never really felt that I had any special gifts. I would compare myself to my younger sister, Karen. I always heard how pretty and creative she was. Karen was an artist and went on to become an outstanding architect after college. The one claim to fame in my family I could brag on myself was being the first daughter to graduate from college, and what a great personality I had. Add that to the fact I was probably the least likely to graduate in the first place, it was more remarkable. My older brother became a fighter pilot. My older sister, Kathryn, has the highest IQ, and Karen has the most creative genes. I'm the middle daughter who had an inferiority complex. Even once I completed college at Texas A&M, I can honestly say I was not sure of what I wanted to do with my degree in health education. When I became disabled my life, my positive attitude and behavior made me stand out, so to speak, in the crowd. When my minister spoke on the above verse, I realized the Holy Spirit is at work in me. I can now make a difference in other lives; whereas, if this had not happened, I may have drifted through life with mediocrity. God is preparing us for major work, perhaps to do something greater than we ever would have accomplished if life was easier. I no longer feel inferior. Perhaps God always knew I was more prepared for this disability. I felt I was a mediocre walking person, but I am an outstanding quadriplegic!

Throughout my book, you could probably detect by now how important my daughters have been in my life; what a blessing they are. I can honestly say I'm not sure how my life would have turned out if Stephen had not remained in the marriage following our car accident and if we had not gone on to have these two beautiful children. Even though he did eventually break apart our family with his actions, I have forgiven him and moved on with a much better perspective. After all, any bitterness on my part would only take away from my growth and happiness. As Philippians 4:13 states, "We can do all things through Christ who strengthens us." Because of the divorce, I became more independent and stronger in my faith. I grew up Catholic and was not raised quoting Bible verses. However, from going to church and observing my parents, I knew God had a plan for me and it was my choice how I decided to carry forth.

I don't believe I'm alone in saying the two toughest things to follow in the Bible are forgiveness and to be thankful for everything, even difficulties or tragedies. But in my life, both have proven to be true. I don't have a crystal ball to know what my life would have been like without the accident, but I know it has been an honor to serve as an example and hopefully a positive influence for someone else. Although I'm sure bitterness was detected in the chapter on my divorce, I hope it did not overshadow everything Stephen did for me in the sixteen years of our marriage. Despite everything that happened with Stephen, I have forgiven him and will always feel grateful for our two daughters.

Do not be afraid. Stand firm, and you will see the deliverance the Lord will bring you today (Exodus 14:13).

This is one of the hardest quotes for me to live by—not relating to my disability but to my daughters' lives. I'm a constant worrier on their behalf. I tell everyone I have a deal with God; since this happened to me, "our" daughters will be safe. However, I know God doesn't make deals. I just tell myself to convince myself that they'll be okay despite all the dangers in the world. We have all been fortunate. Through our prayers and belief in his deliverance, we have been blessed in more ways than I can count. Who would have thought on that fateful day on December 16, 1983, I would go on to have two beautiful daughters and a productive lifestyle?

If anyone finds themselves in my situation, what advice would I give? Of course, it is dependent on many factors. But the two most important for me were to (1) focus day-to-day on small goals and achievements; it would be too easy to get discouraged looking at the big picture and what I could not accomplish. The other is to (2) let go of pride and in some cases, like mine, modesty as well. I had to learn to accept help, to realize with this injury many people were going to be seeing my naked body beside my husband! To this day, I still rely on many people to help me with certain things—to the point of driving my daughters or family members crazy when they visit. But, hey, like I said, "Breaking your neck is a pain in the butt!" I have learned a sense of humor goes a long way in easing the pain. Many people who suffer from a tragedy ask, "Why me?" I believe that is the most common question asked of those who suffer tragedies. Not everyone may find an answer to this question or be satisfied with the answer. I would be lying if I said that being quadriplegic doesn't bother me, but I have accepted the reality and believe I have made more of a difference in the wheelchair than if the accident had not occurred. What sets me apart from others with life's challenges is my positivity. No matter how I may feel on a daily basis, I put forth an effort to smile and "deal with it." Why this happened to me will only be answered through God, but I think it was because I had the inner spirit to inspire others with my attitude and daily behavior in handling my disability. I was told recently my eyes sparkled. As I thought about it later, it goes along with this theory of inner spirit and my ability to project a positive image despite my disability. My Sunday school teacher, Dr. Tim Scott, calls me "joy on wheels." I'm proud to reflect this quality and look forward to meeting Jesus with much joy!

My disability did not limit playtime with Carissa and Cailey.

THOUGHTS ON FAITH
AND PRAYER

Devotionals presented to my church, 1997

One of the questions most frequently asked of me is how I keep such a positive attitude. Although I could probably write a book on this, I have a few experiences to share with you that will hopefully give you some insight:

- It began with my parents, who provided me with a stable, loving childhood. I remember more my mother's smiling eyes than the punishment she dealt out.
- It's got to have something to do with the fact that I survived a car accident when the odds were against me.
- It may be when I was in the rehab hospital in '84 for five months and saw people much worse than I was.
- My attitude always lightens when I see a child's eyes widen and says, "I want to ride that ride," when they see one of my daughters on the back of my chair at the park.
- On one occasion, I recall a little boy's enthusiasm as he watched my van lift operate and then excitedly described to his friends what he had seen.
- How can I not be positive when I looked into Carissa's big blue eyes when she was three years old and she told me in one of my frustrated moments, "You can do it, Mommy!"
- Or in Cailey's dare-all eyes that say, "Catch me if you can!"
- There's always a smiling face waiting to open a door for me, although once when I opened a particularly heavy door on my own and was told I was awesome. Whatever troubles I had that day were forgotten!

- If I'm ever feeling down, all I do is get behind the wheel of my van and turn up the radio to my Oldies station, and within minutes, good memories override any unpleasant ones.
- The greatest gift of positive thinking has been knowing when I can laugh at myself in humble moments, like when I got stuck in the mud up to the axle and Stephen had to lift me out of the chair before he could get it moving again.
- I certainly can't get down when I think of how I got stuck standing up in this chair and my seventy-five-year-old neighbor, with a weak heart, came to my rescue and offered to lift me out of the chair before I passed out!
- Finally. How in the world, with all the progress they're making in medical advances, can I give up hope now? The best is yet to come!

Devotional, June 20, 1999

When Cailey says her prayers each night, she prays that I will be able to walk someday. One night, she did what she had the talent for doing—she stumped me with one of her profound questions. She looked at me with all the seriousness of a six-year-old pondering one of life's tough questions and asked me when I was going to get up and test to see if her prayers were working! She wanted to know, as so many do, if her faith was paying off with results!

I attended the series on Larry Dossey's book *Healing Words* that Linda McDermont did during Lent, and although the book didn't really answer my questions about prayer and healing, I collected some interesting quotes that I'd like to share with you today.

"Awe is a way of being in rapport with the mystery of all reality. Something sacred is at stake in every moment" (A. Heschel).

The real healing is in our connectedness with God.

"Penetrating so many secrets, we cease to believe in the unknowable. But there it sits, nevertheless, calmly licking its chops" (H. L. Mencken)

"God is a sphere whose center is everywhere and whose circumference is nowhere" (Humes Trismegistus)

"Everyone prays in their own language, and there is no language that God does not understand" (Duke Ellington)

"Pray as you can, not as you can't" (Don Chapman).

And my favorite that described the ambiguity of the book: "There is no answer; there never has been an answer; there never will be an answer; that's the answer" (Gertrude Stein).

FAMILY PERSPECTIVES

Written by Carissa, June 14, 2016

You know when you're a kid and everyone tells you to make a wish for your birthday? Well, every time I had the opportunity to make a wish, I wished as hard as I could that my mom would somehow walk again. It took me a while to realize that it would take some serious scientific and physical breakthroughs, but I still pray for a miracle anyway. But I also realized that maybe my mom's miracle was living through the trauma and waking up every day with a positive outlook. She brings so much light to the people around her. She's now a Stephen's Minister. She and Angel are like a duo who bring smiles to everyone who meets them.

My mom was two years younger than me when she was told she would never walk again. So young and just starting her adult life. She loved to run, ride horses and swim. I can't imagine the strength she had to muster not just all those years ago, but every day. With the scary things going on in this world people like my mom embody what it's like to love and forgive. It's people like her who remind us to stay positive and focused on the people doing good in the world. Love is love, no matter which way you look at it. None of us have any idea how long we will be on this earth, but I'll do my best to make most of it and hopefully have a fraction of the impact my mom has had.

Can you imagine being told at the age of 25 that you would never walk again? I can't fathom the fear, pain and unknown my mom experienced in the weeks following her car accident all those years ago. One of the first things she asked during her rehab was whether she would still be able to have children. Once she realized the possibility of raising a family still existed, she set her eyes on that goal and never looked back.

She started with a wound that she thought would never heal, but she decided to let the light in.

I'm so amazed every day at her strength to carry on. Without her faith and positive attitude, I would not be here today. I would not be a mama raising my own son. I have never seen my mom commit a selfish act or ask, "Why me?" No matter the circumstance, my mom has found a way to overcome it. Now as a new mom, I can't believe the extra steps my mom had to go through to take care of me! My mom worked AND pumped/ breastfed me for a year. At 7 months, I found nursing a challenge, and I have the complete use of my hands and fingers!

It is true that when you become a mom you really do appreciate your mother even more. I have always been amazed by her, but now I have a new appreciation for what she went through to make me feel as normal as possible. Growing up, I didn't know any other way. When kids looked at my mom's ramp that came out of her van they said, "WOAH, that looks like a spaceship!" and they watched in wonder as I rode my mom's chair and zoomed around the mall. I thought that's what everyone else's childhood was like too! I never concentrated on the fact that my mom couldn't kick a soccer ball around with me. I just knew that she was there to watch every game and every practice and that's all that mattered to me.

Her strength speaks volumes. Mom, I can't thank you enough for the sacrifices you made for me. I know you feel like you can't do everything Bon and Grandad do for Connor, but he is going to have his own special bond with you. I can't wait for him to request the "Wheelchair express!" and show off to all his friends his Gigi's awesome "spaceship" van!

We love you! Forever our mama (and Gigi) you'll be.

Bob Dixon, March 2020

After reading this book you will know what an amazing sister I have in Cherie. What you don't know is she was a wonderful, loving person well before her accident. The tragic accident in late 1983 brought the best of her to all of us.

Jo Ella, Clay and I lived in Phoenix at the time of Cherie's accident. The last year before Cherie's accident was tumultuous with the sudden death of my father at a young age. When I received the phone call about Cherie's accident, I didn't really know what to expect. Jo and Clay were already in Texas for a family Christmas. The drive back to Texas by myself gave me time to reflect on my relationship with my sister and wonder about her future. When I first saw her in the Harris Hospital, she was tied to a Stryker bed and was upside down in the bed… Wow! At this point I knew things were more serious than I first thought. Little did I know about all the wonderful events that would occur from such a tragic event.

You can read for yourself all the episodes that followed over that last 38 years. Here is what I know. My sister Cherie is a special person and despite the challenges she faced, she persevered and made a wonderful life for herself and influenced many lives along the way. I couldn't have done what she did… She did do it and I love her more each day for what she had done and who she is.

Kathryn Hughes, March 2020

The very first time I saw Cherie after her injury was in the rehab facility. I was a bit apprehensive, as I had only heard about her time in the hospital. I had Molly with me, who was about 18 months old and still in diapers. Well! I couldn't believe how cheerful she was, even though her poor scalp had not gotten back to normal and so neither had her hair, which kind of stuck out in various directions. Then, a nurse came in to "change her diaper." That is when Molly discovered as she watched the procedure, that, as far as she was concerned, she had the coolest aunt in the universe.

The other thing that stands out to me is how so many people were there for her, not just in the beginning, but throughout her years in Ft. Worth. This tells me as much about Cherie, as it tells me about her friends and acquaintances.

She has the kind of personality and character that people develop a COMMITTED friendship with.

Just the fact that she went back to work in 6 months or so, and went on to have two beautiful daughters demonstrates a willingness not to dwell on the past or what can't be changed, but rather to accept the challenges and LIVE HER LIFE!

I am so in awe of Cherie—of her consistently cheerful attitude, her concern for others, and her STRENGTH. When I am having a difficult day, I simply think of her and how just getting out of bed and ready for the day is a challenge.

I am so proud to call her my sister.

Karen Dixon, March 2020

I will never forget the night the phone rang, and it was my mom tearfully telling me that Cherie had been in a terrible car accident. She was paralyzed. The first time I saw Cherie in the hospital she was on a Stryker Frame a strange device that keeps your spine immobilized. I can only describe it as looking like something you use to torture people. They flip this contraption over from time to time so sometimes she was facing up and sometimes facing down. When I came to visit, Cherie was facing down. She was in great spirits as I am sure at this point, she was heavily sedated. I laid on the floor looking up and we visited for a long time, we laughed, we cried, we prayed for better days.

The next visit she had been moved to an actual bed, but this bed rotated side to side very slowly so every so often you would have to run around to the other side to continue your chat. Again, Cherie was in good spirits and as usual was trying to make all of us feel better. We laughed more this time, we cried a little and prayed for better days.

After a while Cherie was moved to a rehab facility. I got on a plane and flew to Dallas to see her. So many things were going through my head; would she be the same person I had grown up with? We were always very close. All my fears were dispelled when I saw her that day. She was the same person, she just had some limitations now, but I will tell you she did not ever let those limitations stop her from doing something she wanted to do. Those early days were so hard, but she did not let that get in her way. We laughed a lot that day, I don't remember any tears. We were beginning to see better days ahead.

When people first meet Cherie, she always has a smile and positive attitude, which makes them want to help her. But once they KNOW her, they come to realize she is helping them. Helping them see the good in the world even though the world can turn in ways we don't expect. Helping them find a smile even if they are having a bad day. Helping them know that God has a purpose for us even if we are not always sure what that purpose is. There are so many stories to tell of Cherie's struggles, but I will leave those details to her. It has been a crazy ride down a road with more twist and turns than you can imagine. Cherie has navigated that road with determination, perseverance and faith, all with a beautiful smile that sometimes makes you forget everything else.

ACKNOWLEDGMENTS

There are not enough words to describe my appreciation to my family, who have always been there for me. Even before my car accident, I knew they could be depended upon when I needed them. But when my world turned upside down—and I mean literally when I was in the hospital Stryker bed and they would lie on the floor to visit me—I was surrounded by love and support. This has continued throughout my journey, both emotionally and financially. There is an ongoing byplay with my brother-in-law Tom on how much in debt I am in with all the household projects he has done for me. The latest was an automatic door, which is totally awesome and whose installation proved to be a thorn in his side. I let him know I would never get out of debt with the time and frustration this cost him!

In my life, I have had many blessings surround me. It comes from the circumstances in my life and would be impossible to name everyone; however, I would like to take this opportunity to express gratitude to friends; church family; and all the services which helped in my rehabilitation—doctors, nurses, and caregivers. I praise God every single day for these blessings and for granting me the strength and courage to handle this disability and the path He chose for me.

Although it has taken longer than expected, I could not have succeeded in completing the book without Gillian Hill, Jerrie Comstock, Donnis Baggett for help editing my manuscript and Covenant Books for editing and publishing my book.

A TRIBUTE TO ALL
MY CAREGIVERS

No one has ever seen God; but if we love one another, God lives in us, and his love is made complete in us (1 John 4:12).

I see this come alive all the time with the people in my life, especially those who take care of me. I can't say enough about the role that caregivers play in my life. I literally cannot make it a single day without them to help me get up in the morning and then help put me to bed every night. I like to think I am independent through the day, but it would be impossible to start it or end it without their assistance. Simple tasks such as rolling out of bed and showering for the day, taken for granted when I was walking, are now planned activities that all require a minimum of forty-five minutes to one hour.

Of the thirty-six years I have been in the wheelchair, I have had to hire caregivers for about twenty years. Stephen was my caregiver for the sixteen years we were married; however, once we divorced, it was essential to hire *reliable* caregivers. During the interview, I always stressed if the individual does not show up, I don't get up! I also stressed if they do not arrive on time, I, in turn, would not get to work on time. It's a simple domino effect.

I have been incredibly blessed with caring and dependable caregivers. My first caregiver was Maria. She was caring and proficient in her duties for ten years. I think a caregiver's job is extremely demanding and often can be taken for granted and consequently leads to job burnout faster than most other jobs. To relieve stress on Maria, I hired Sol, who was primarily my evening caregiver but would save me anytime Maria could not be there. After Maria left, Sol took over both morning and evening duties. She became like a part of our family, which is true of most caregivers.

Another special person to enter my life was Cynthia Whitley, who was my evening caregiver for four years. Unfortunately, she had a terrible accident on the way to my house one evening and was out of commission for over a year. I felt horrible for her circumstances, because she was coming to help me. We stayed in touch while I was in Houston, and she continued to help me on occasion.

The hardest part of deciding to leave Houston to move to College Station in 2013 was leaving my caregivers of three years, Lucilla (mornings) and Ana Lila (evenings and weekend mornings). They both were the most loving and reliable caregivers a person could ever wish to find. I could set my clock by the timing of Lucilla, who arrived exactly at five o'clock every weekday for three years! If I was late for work, it could never be blamed on her. One of my pet peeves before and following my disability is clutter. It was my habit to clean up before my housekeeper, Victoria, came. I would chance being late to work rather than leave Cailey's clothes on the floor. My service dog, Angel, knew I didn't like soccer shoes and jerseys left on the floor and would often pick them up before being commanded to do it. There were many tears shed between my dear caregivers and housekeeper before I moved. My only hope was they all felt treasured and needed.

My biggest fear in moving to College Station was finding as great caregivers as I left behind in Houston. I was fortunate that an agency I had used in California when I visited my daughter Cailey at Berkeley had an office in College Station. Visiting Angels was also the only agency in town who would allow caregivers to work a minimum of one hour per shift. Amanda, my first "Angel" sent, proved to be just that. She stayed a year, often doing the day and night shift and always with a caring attitude, and continued to help when I was in a bind. Presently, I give big kudos to Bielka, who took over when Amanda left. I can't express enough appreciation to this amazing woman who also has come mornings and evenings without a complaint and a warm, loving spirit. She is four feet eleven, is stronger than she looks, and has a feisty attitude that I love! I finally got her some relief by getting Visiting Angels back in here for three mornings a week, which brought Elizabeth into my life, who is loving and attentive to my meticulous needs. It's nice to utilize an agency because they can be dependable about screening and hiring quality caregivers. This has been my experience at least with both Amanda and Elizabeth. Presently my team consists of Bielka and Elizabeth covering the mornings, Elizabeth covering the weeknights and Patti instrumental in covering most weekends and as backup.

I can't stress enough how important all my caregivers have been and still are to me. I always strive to communicate this appreciation when they have worked or are still working for me. I hope this tribute in my book to them will help express their value and meaning in my life. I tip my hat to all caregivers! I have been blessed with great ones! Visiting Angels, Signature Select Services, Maria, Cynthia, Sol, Victoria, Lucilla, Ana Lila, Amanda, Bielka, Elizabeth, Sheri, Patti, Mary, Summer, Kelsey, and Tonya.

NOTES

[1] A pulmonary embolism (PE) is a blockage of the main artery of the lung or one of its branches by a substance that has travelled from elsewhere in the body through the bloodstream (embolism). PE most commonly results from deep vein thrombosis (a blood clot in the deep veins of the legs or pelvis) that breaks off and migrates to the lung, a process termed venous thromboembolism (VTE).

Symptoms of pulmonary embolism include difficulty breathing, chest pain on inspiration, and palpitations. Clinical signs include low blood oxygen saturation and cyanosis, rapid breathing, and a rapid heart rate. Severe cases of PE can lead to collapse, abnormally low blood pressure, and sudden death (Goldhaber S. Z., "Pulmonary Thromboembolism." In Kasper DL, Braunwald E, Fauci AS, et. al. Harrison's Principles of Internal Medicine (16th ed.). New York, NY: McGraw-Hill. pp. 1561–65. ISBN 0-07-139140-1).

[2] Quadriplegia is a condition of paralysis in which a person loses complete or partial use of all limbs and the torso. Also known as tetraplegia, this type of paralysis involves sensory and motor loss, which means that the victim has lost both sensation and control. Quadriplegia occurs when the brain, neck, or spinal cord is severely damaged; but it can also be the result of certain illnesses, including cancer, osteoporosis, and multiple sclerosis.

More than 250,000 Americans have suffered debilitating spinal cord injuries, with 52 percent of them being paraplegic and 47 percent being quadriplegic. Each year, more than 11,000 people suffer spinal cord injuries that leave them paraplegic or quadriplegic, of which 82 percent are male, and 56 percent of these injuries are suffered by people ages sixteen through thirty. The average age of a person who suffers this spinal injury is thirty-one years old.

There are eight classifications of quadriplegia in relation to spinal cord injuries, graded C-1 through C-8 and based on the impacted and affected vertebrae.

C-1, C-2, and C-3: These classifications each involve limited head and neck movement based on the muscle strength of the individual; and the person will suffer complete paralysis of the body, legs, and arms. The victim will require assistance in every detail of his daily life, from eating and drinking to changing clothes and getting into bed. Regular travel would be conducted in an electric wheelchair that would be controlled by either a chin control, depending on the neck and head strength, or a breathing straw. The person will require assistance in breathing through a respirator or ventilator, as well as with coughing and clearing blockages of the throat. Speech impairments will require the use of a computer.

C-4: This classification is almost entirely similar to a C-1, C-2, or C-3 injury, in that the victim will require assistance in all daily activities, including washing, dressing, bathroom use, travel, and eating and drinking. The victim also uses a motorized wheelchair that is powered by either chin movement, depending on the muscle strength for head and neck movement, or a breathing straw apparatus. However, the difference between a C-4 injury and a C-1, 2, or 3 is the person will have control of his or her own breathing with a C-4.

C-5: With this spinal injury, the victim maintains head and neck movement, as well as partial shoulder movement depending on the upper body strength of the individual. The body and legs are completely paralyzed, and the wrists and fingers will have no movement. However, there will be flexing ability in the elbows and hands. This leaves open the possibility for feeding oneself and controlling menial tasks such as brushing teeth or shaving with the assistance of special straps. Breathing is done without a ventilator; however, all regular daily activities will still require assistance.

C-6: The C-6 injury mirrors most of the aspects of the C-5 injury, including good head, neck, and shoulder strength. However, the difference is that the C-6 injury allows additional voluntary wrist and elbow movement. With this injury, the victim can complete some tasks through assistance, such as shaving, brushing teeth, and eating, but can also handle some partial dressing duties. However, all other daily routines require complete assistance.

C-7 and C-8: With these specific injuries, the victim will have no body and leg movement but good head, neck, and shoulder movement, as well as full elbow and wrist use, and partial finger movement. The person will need partial assistance with most routine activities depending on physical strength and volume of hand and arm movement. Wheelchair travel is a bit easier and with the proper equipment, a C-7 or C-8 victim can even operate a motor vehicle. The main difference between C-7 and C-8 injuries is that C-7 injuries most often allow the use of the thumb.

Quadriplegia can also be caused by damages to the thoracic nerve segments (T1-T10), lumbar nerves (L1-L5), and sacral nerves (S1-S5).

Paraplegia is paralysis characterized by motor or sensory loss in the lower limbs and trunk. Approximately 11,000 spinal cord injuries reported each year in the United States involve paraplegia. Such injuries commonly result from automobile and motorcycle accidents, sporting accidents, falls, and gunshot wounds. (Resource on Spinal Cord Injuries).

[3] Greenfield filter: a filter placed in the inferior vena cava under fluoroscopic (X-ray-like) guidance. It is used in patients who are particularly vulnerable to pulmonary embolism, such as those diagnosed with deep venous thrombosis with contraindications to anticoagulation, to prevent venous emboli from entering the pulmonary circulation (Mosby's Medical Dictionary, 8th edition. © 2009, Elsevier).

[4] Autonomic dysreflexia (AD), also known as autonomic hyperreflexia, is a potentially life-threatening condition which can be considered a medical

emergency requiring immediate attention. AD occurs most often in spinal cord–injured individuals with spinal lesions above the T6 spinal cord level; although, it has been known to occur in patients with a lesion as low as T10 (Valles, M., Benito, J. E., Vidal, J., "Cerebral Hemorrhage Due to Autonomic Dysreflexia in a Spinal Cord Injury Patient." Spinal Cord 43: 738-740).

Acute autonomic dysreflexia is a reaction of the autonomic (involuntary) nervous system to overstimulation. It is characterized by severe paroxysmal hypertension (episodic high blood pressure) associated with throbbing headaches, profuse sweating, nasal stuffiness, flushing of the skin above the level of the lesion, bradycardia, apprehension, and anxiety which is sometimes accompanied by cognitive impairment (Khastgir, Jay, Marcus J. Drake, and Paul Abrams, "Recognition and Effective Management of Autonomic Dysreflexia in Spinal Cord Injuries." Expert Opinion on Pharmacotherapy 8, no. 7 (2007): 945–56. https://doi.org/10.1517/14656566.8.7.945).

[5] Radial keratotomy (RK) is a refractive surgical procedure to correct myopia (nearsightedness) that was developed in 1974 by Svyatoslav Fyodorov, a Russian ophthalmologist. It has been largely supplanted by newer operations, such as photorefractive keratectomy, LASIK, Epi-LASIK and the phakic intraocular lens.

[6] Hypothyroidism poses a special danger to newborns and infants. A lack of thyroid hormones in the system at an early age can lead to the development of cretinism (mental retardation) and dwarfism (stunted growth). Most infants now have their thyroid levels checked routinely soon after birth.

[7] Pregnancy statistics: each year about two thousand women of childbearing age in the United States have a spinal cord injury. Only a few mostly anecdotal reports describe pregnancy after such an injury. In a retrospective study of sixteen women with a spinal cord injury, half of whom have a complete injury and about half quadriplegia, twenty-five pregnancies occurred, with twenty-one carried to full term. The women delayed pregnancy an average of 6.5 years after their injury, with an average age at first pregnancy of 26.8 years. Cesarean section was necessary in four patients because of inadequate progress of labor. In five deliveries, an episiotomy and local anesthesia were required; seven required epidural anesthesia, including all Cesarean sections; and ten did not require anesthesia. Several complications have been identified in the antepartum, intrapartum, and postpartum periods including autonomic hyperreflexia, premature labor, pressure sores, urinary tract infections, abnormal presentation, and failure to progress. Ultrasonography and amniocentesis were used selectively. Women with spinal cord injuries can have healthy children, although there are significant risks, and these women have special needs (Cross, L. L., Meythaler, J. M., Tuel, S. M., and Cross, A. L., "Pregnancy Following Spinal Cord Injury." The Western Journal of Medicine [1991]: 607–611).

ABOUT THE AUTHOR

Cherie Cotner is a quadriplegic who broke her neck due to a spinal cord injury at the age of twenty-five and persevered through recovery to go back to work and raise two children. She currently resides in College Station, Texas, the home of her beloved Texas Aggies. Although retired, she remains active in her church as a Stephen Minister and volunteers with her service dog, Vancouver with Aggieland Pets with a Purpose. She also continues advocating for Service Dogs Inc. In her spare time, she enjoys visiting her grandchildren, Connor and Elsie, as often as possible.